Rob Silverstone spent many years as a chef in kitchens in Oxford, Nice and Copenhagen.

He became a university lecturer in food and nutrition, and later opened a seafront restaurant in an arch beneath Brighton prom. Fish straight from the fishermen and organic sheep cheese from the farm.

It was this attraction for authentic produce that took him to Normandy, and he is now back in Brighton with 'The Little Farmhouse Deli.'

A MULE
IN ROUEN

A DISCOVERY OF
UPPER NORMANDY

To Iain,

Happy trekking
in Normandy

[signature]

Rob Silverstone

A Mule in Rouen

A Discovery of Upper Normandy

Vanguard Press

A CIP catalogue record for this title is
available from the British Library
ISBN 1 84386 163 1

*Vanguard Press is an imprint of
Pegasus Elliot MacKenzie Publishers Ltd.*
www.pegasuspublishers.com

First Published in 2004
Revised Edition 2004

**Vanguard Press
Sheraton House Castle Park
Cambridge England**

Printed & Bound in Great Britain

Dedication

To:
Basile Basilovich
Madame Bezzer
And La Belle Baleine

Table of Contents

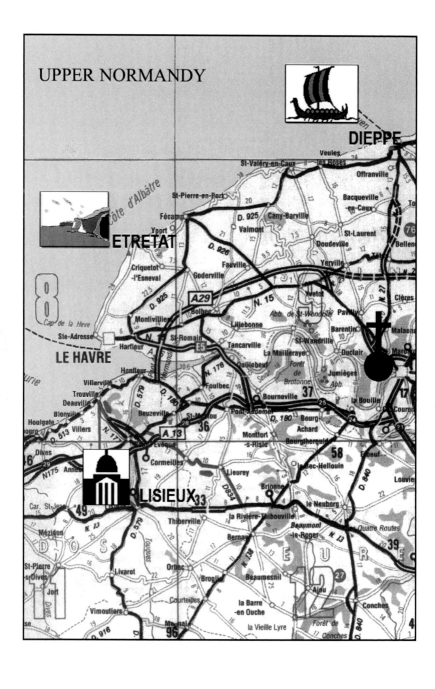

UPPER NORMANDY

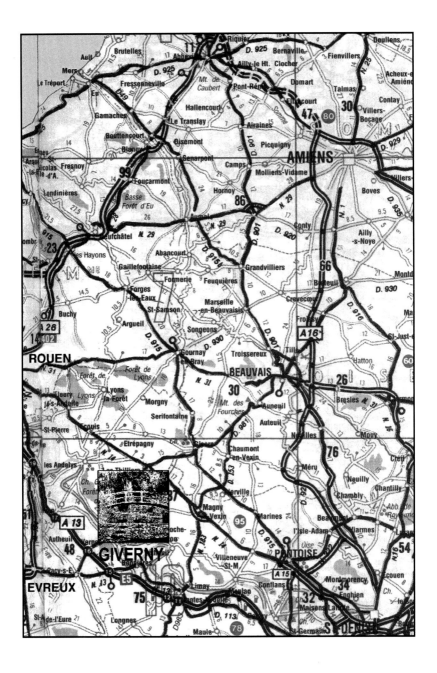

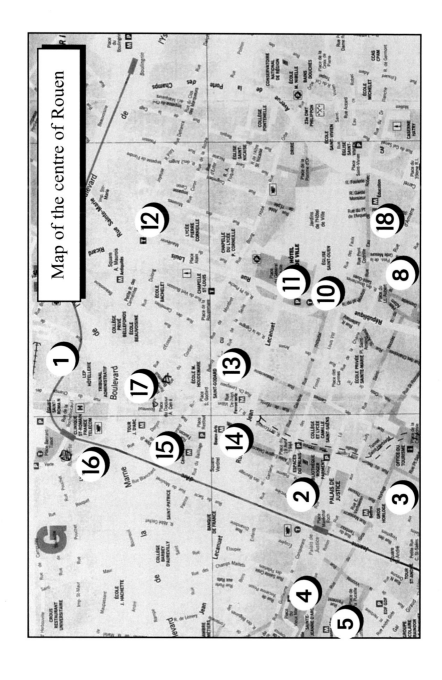

Map of the centre of Rouen

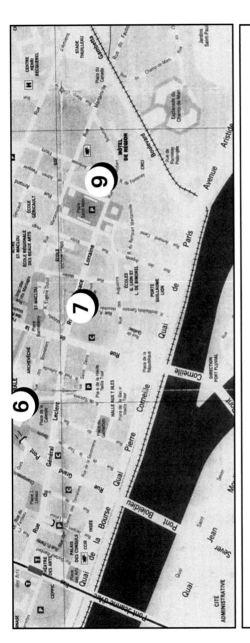

1. Gare Rive Droite Station
2. Palais de Justice
3. Gros Horloge
4. Place de Vieux Marché, et l'église Jeanne d'Arc
5. Hôtel de Bourgtheroulde
6. Cathédrale
7. Église Saint Maclou. Antique dealer district
8. École des Beaux-Arts
9. Place St. Marc - Sunday Market
10. Abbé St. Rouen
11. Town Hall
12. Musée d'Antiquités
13. Iron Works Museum - Musée Ferronerie
14. Musée Beaux Arts - main town museum
15. Musée Céramique
16. Café Métropole
17. Le Donjon - Dungeon
18. Rue Eau de Robec

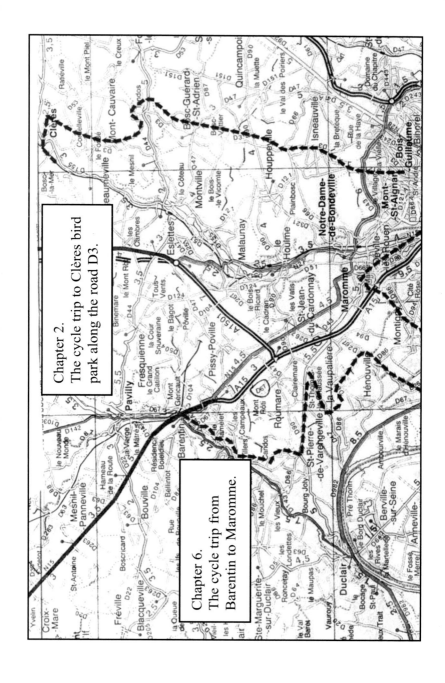

Chapter 2.
The cycle trip to Clères bird park along the road D3.

Chapter 6.
The cycle trip from Barentin to Maromme.

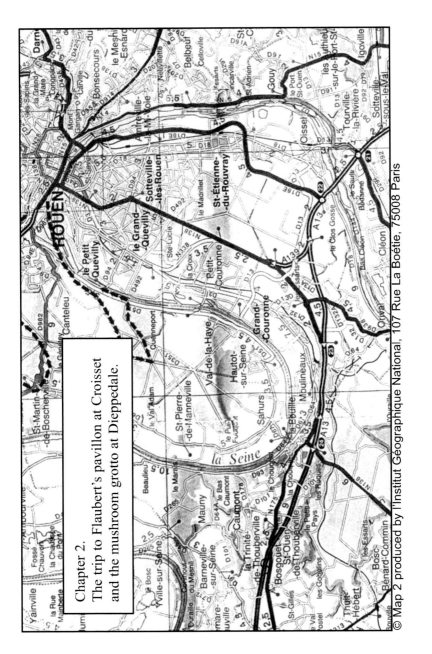

Chapter 2.
The trip to Flaubert's pavillon at Croisset and the mushroom grotto at Dieppedale.

© Map 2 produced by l'Institut Géographique National, 107 Rue La Boétie, 75008 Paris

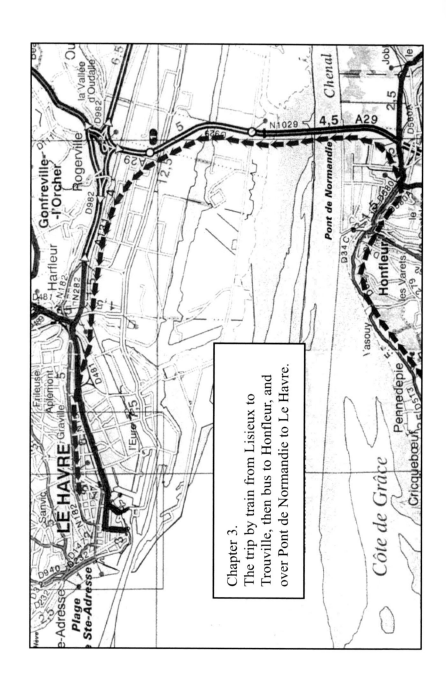

Chapter 3.
The trip by train from Lisieux to Trouville, then bus to Honfleur, and over Pont de Normandie to Le Havre.

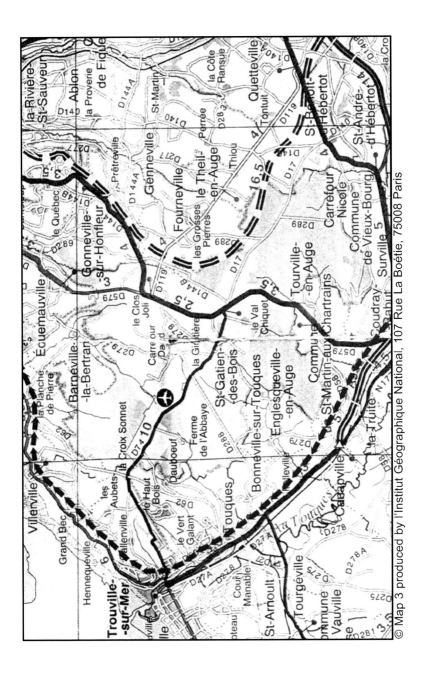

© Map 3 produced by l'Institut Géographique National, 107 Rue La Boétie, 75008 Paris

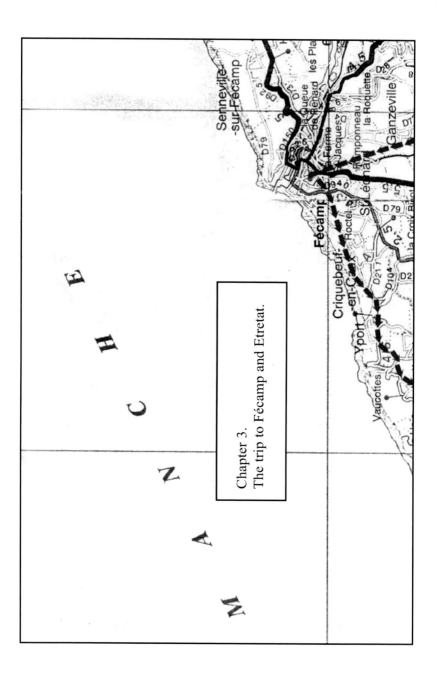

Chapter 3.
The trip to Fécamp and Etretat.

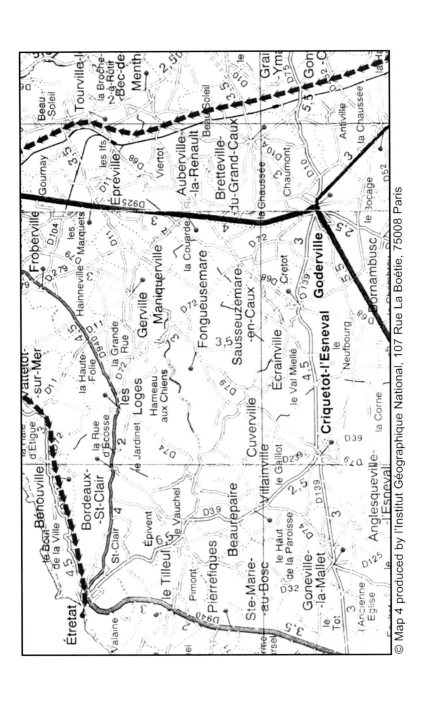

© Map 4 produced by l'Institut Géographique National, 107 Rue La Boétie, 75008 Paris

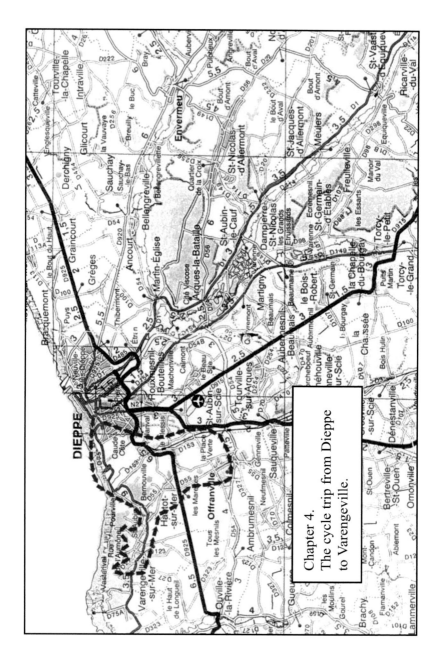

Chapter 4.
The cycle trip from Dieppe
to Varengeville.

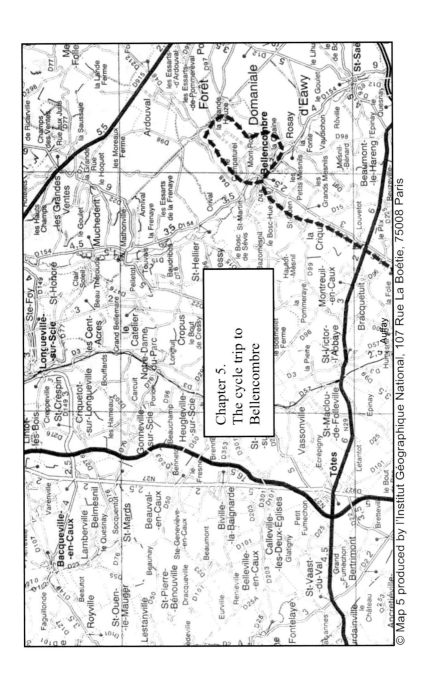

Chapter 5.
The cycle trip to Bellencombre

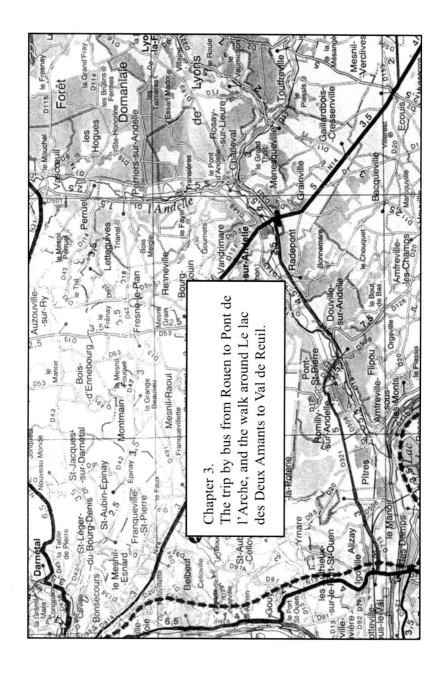

Chapter 3.
The trip by bus from Rouen to Pont de l'Arche, and the walk around Le lac des Deux Amants to Val de Reuil.

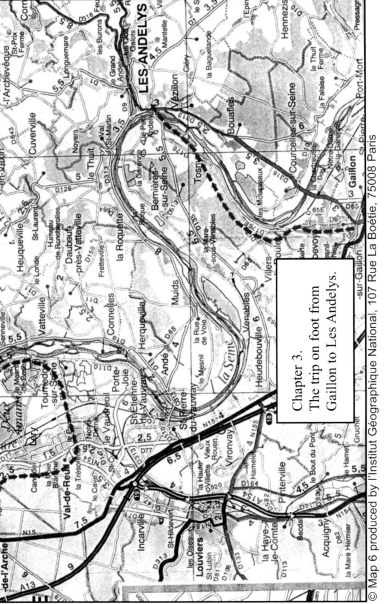

Chapter 3.
The trip on foot from
Gaillon to Les Andelys.

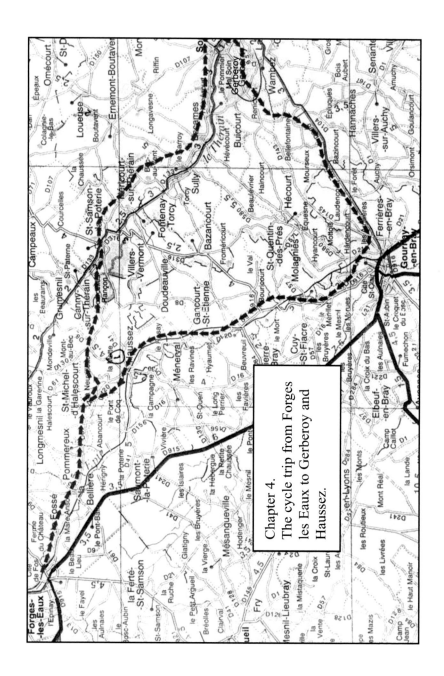

Chapter 4.
The cycle trip from Forges
les Eaux to Gerberoy and
Haussez.

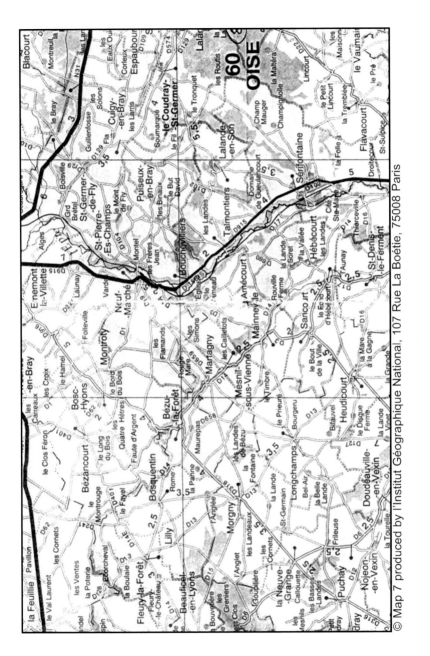

© Map 7 produced by l'Institut Géographique National, 107 Rue La Boétie, 75008 Paris

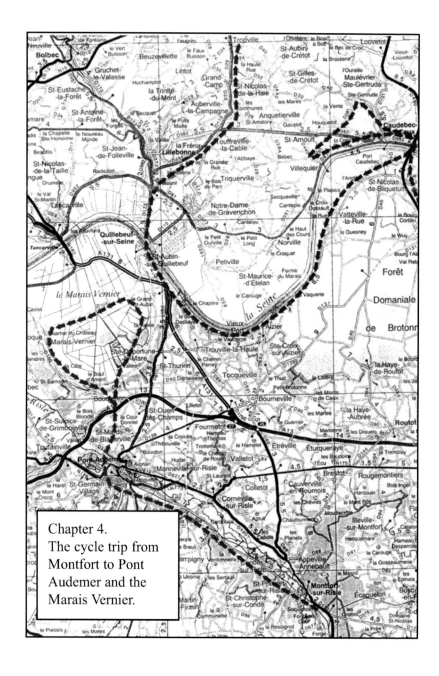

Chapter 4.
The cycle trip from
Montfort to Pont
Audemer and the
Marais Vernier.

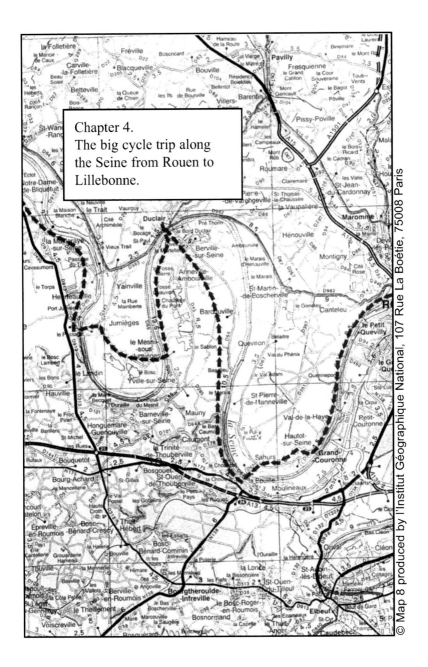

Chapter 4.
The big cycle trip along
the Seine from Rouen to
Lillebonne.

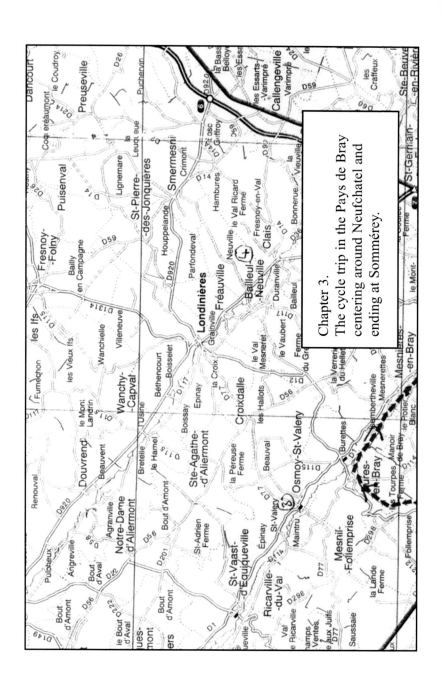

Chapter 3.
The cycle trip in the Pays de Bray centering around Neufchatel and ending at Somméry.

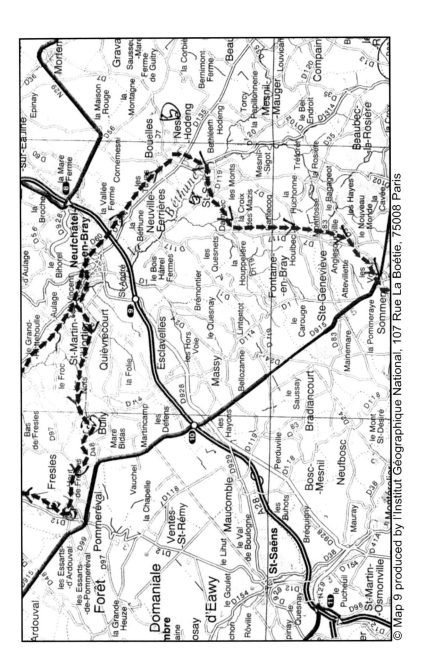

© Map 9 produced by l'Institut Géographique National, 107 Rue La Boétie, 75008 Paris

Chapter One

Getting There

Living in Brighton, the French connection is supplied by the oldest Channel crossing, between Newhaven and Dieppe. Newhaven is an anonymous place, with nothing to commend it, other than as embarkation point for France. Dieppe on the other hand, has a fishing fleet bringing in scallops, mussels and squid, a score of seafood restaurants, a dinky little Abbey, a museum perched high on the cliff top within the castle walls, and a Saturday market to die for. Across Europe, in the most beguiling places, markets tend to be replica stall cities – Fruit of the Loom, net curtains and cut price face flannels. Dieppe is distinctive. All the Normandy countryside comes to town, with local cheeses, honeys, twenty varieties of awesome sausage, stalls abundant in salad and vegetables. And of course every form of produce that can emanate from the Apple.

Until the early 1990's, the crossing was very much a meeting of two state railways, SNCF/Sealink. The London train took you right to the ferry terminal, and at Dieppe the boat inched deep into the quayside, to be met by the Paris train, clanking its way across the streets and dockside. All that has changed now. There is no longer any synchrony between boat and train. The ferry port has moved from its picturesque setting among cafés and restaurants, to an austere, cement berth out of town. Ownership of the ferry company has changed several times, and somehow the crossing seems to have lost its sense of identity.

Every February I used to take a group of about 20 catering students over to Dieppe. Eminent educational grounds were established for Brighton University to subsidise the trip, but basically it was an excuse for a good time. One year I awoke to find the student body heinously hung-over. Determined not to waste the day, I left them sleeping in their pits, and ventured out of the little hotel. Dieppe is a town of sea mists and hanging rain, and that morning was particularly uninviting. There is a Pissaro painting, 'The fair at Dieppe-a sunny afternoon', where the sky appears distinctly grey, so you will understand that when there is no hint of sunshine, Dieppe is deeply guttering grey. Yet despite the logic of a return beneath the duvet, something impelled me to the station and the train for Rouen.

In many towns they've preserved a bit of the past as a picturesque tourist attraction. Brighton's Lanes are typical of this, a small network of alleyways, full of boutiques and antique shops, but totally uninhabited by the local people. Rouen is so different. A large part of the town still comprises sloping old Norman houses, fronted with thick timbers. All very much lived-in and served by the multitude of tradesmen that existed in Britain prior to the monolithic high street chains. I wandered round the narrow, cobbled streets, enchanted by the lopsided buildings and the little garret flats beneath the rooftops.

One side of the Rue Jeanne d'Arc ends up at a long square lined with restaurants and patisseries. In the middle is a food market and a bizarre, modern church, built on its side, the spire stretching along the ground. Step inside and there is a rare quality of warmth. On the other side of the Rue Jeanne d'Arc there is stunning civic architecture. The Palais de Justice and l'Hôtel de Ville impress both with their size and artistic flourish. Then you discover the lovely old buildings and restored theatre on the Place Rougemare. The museum buildings with secluded gardens, one leading to a torrent of fountains among ramshackle statues. Inside the Musée des Beaux Arts is a great amphitheatre of a room, sky-lit, as tall as the building itself, with three huge Raoul Dufy paintings and a vast mural by Jules Alexandre Grun. You can sit there, tranquil and pleasantly overwhelmed.

Which is something of the sentiment upon discovering Rouen Cathedral. You approach it along the pedestrianised Rue du Gros Horloge, which contains a unique old clock on a little bridge, wonderfully painted and sculpted. At the end is the Cathedral, powerful, ornate, steepling high into the sky. When later I came to make Rouen my winter home, I would be drawn to this place every day. Understand, the Cathedral holds no religous appeal for me. Atheism is one of the few ideals left intact over time. But the beauty of this building, the scale of the work conducted simply with pulleys and scaffolding, chisels and hammers. Over centuries. It dominates every aspect of the town and occupies a place inside your mind.

I returned to Dieppe with a secret discovery. The students were stirring. We went out to eat.

***

Well the deed is done. Fell off the ferry and into the savings bank, et voilà my first instalment for the Rouen flat safely deposited. This corner of Normandy is quite familiar to me now. Made my way directly to the boulangerie where they bake the most perfect seigle aux noix et raisins – such a tasty, wholemeal morsel in this land of sugared apples, butter and cream. Then onto Rouen, and the little Hotel Morand close beside La Musée des Beaux Arts, with its quiet street and rarely sumptuous breakfast-preserves not in plastic, unadulterated yoghurt, limitless juice and coffee. Best of all is the Café de la Grande Poste, which must be the most wondrous café in the world. The waiters know what they're doing, the glasses shine, prices are reasonable, but it is the decor that really impresses. Tables of solid wood, fluted and smooth at the edge, and not a hint of a wobble as I write these lines. Exquisitely etched windows and sparkling mirrors. Classical paintings look down on you from the ceiling, the floor is like worn marble. Last night, General de Gaulle and Gerard Depardieu ate here, separately and a little the worse for wear. De Gaulle with a dark line from his beak to his deep-set eye. The waiter performed a little Chaplin routine with his hat and cane as the General prepared to leave. Much rummaging of ancient tissues in and out of his pockets, before he was finally up and away.

Sunday, absolutely Deadsville in France, so decide to mosey on up to Paris for the one day of the week when the traffic verges on the humane. The sky is blue, but bitingly cold, one of those forgotten winter days when sunlight offers zilch in warmth rating, stones crack, bones ache and even tramps piss loses its pungency. Stride the length of the Champs Elysée, the pavements colonised by tourists, cars sweeping along regally on the cobbled road. Trees and lawn give way to cafés and boutiques as the Arc de Triomphe approaches. I haven't walked this stretch since over on a socialist youth convention, with Kathy Waxman, aged about 16. We had escaped the intense discussions of the conference hall to hide away in a cinema on the Champs Elysées. I wonder what became of Kathy, or her best friend Elana who went out with Hervé, the French cadre, who had a hook instead of a hand.

Anyway, one of the marvels of Paris, just one turning off the Arc de Triomphe, and you're into narrow streets full of grocers, neighbourhood restaurants, tiny offices and ateliers – the phenomenon of an inhabited inner city. Ambled along happily, and then turning one corner, bonk, there was the Eiffel Tower proclaiming 399 days till the year 2000. People are getting excited about it. I think I'll have to plan some little event of my own back in Brighton. There's something primal about seeing in the Millennium beside the sea.

***

Just when the French expedition is imminent, P&O withdraw the fast ferry, followed swiftly by ugly rumours that the whole Channel link to Dieppe may be cut! Anyway, decide to ignore this doom-laden paper talk, and proceed with plan to purchase modest château in Normandy. The days leading up to the crossing were ominously stormy, and I embarked with some trepidation upon the ferry. The water shimmered menacingly in the mad moonlight as the vessel edged out of its berth, past the Dutch schooner that had recently been dashed against the rocks, bisecting shoals of mackerel surging exhausted into the harbour. Racing clouds obliterated the moon, lightning danced above the railway tracks, and the ferry proceeded relentlessly out into the open sea.

Lay prone in a semi-soporific stupor for the five hours of the crossing. Vaguely aware of the acrid contents of a railway 'salmon sandwich' in my stomach, and two monumental crashes of crockery which must certainly have tipped the economic balance against P&O continuing the Newhaven operation. But proudly produced no projectile of my own, despite the tempest, and strode forth from the terminal at 3.00 am, into the wild night. Dieppe totally deserted, all tucked up against the storm. I booked into l'Hôtel de la Plage for the deep comfort of crisp sheets, a shower, and patting the old bod dry on a pristine towel.

Next morning, over my croissant and prunes, mused that there must surely have been scope for a

Bunuel film to ridicule the French habit of brightly and politely greeting every customer as they enter a shop, café or hotel vestibule, and fastening a fond farewell as they depart. It is just not humanly possible to be pleasant to the whole maelstrom of humanity that crosses ones' portals. And this in a nation otherwise famous for its upturned nose 'quelle con' attitude. The only time an element of edge gets into the voice, is when you get the response wrong, mistaking morning for afternoon, or calling a mademoiselle 'madame'. Given that we're in a sizeable town, not some incestuous hamlet where everyone knows exactly who sired who, how are you meant to know if the shop assistant is married, a mademoiselle or a spent spinster?? Obviously vigilance to the ring-bearing finger is the key.

In Rouen for lunch, and crispy-skinned duck with braised endive for the princely sum of a fiver. Never before had I enjoyed endive, finding it too bitter, but the slow, moist cooking had got rid of this edge, imparting a slightly artichoke flavour, and a wonderful soft texture. And tonight more upmarket, faded embroidery and paintings like in my grandma's Czech dining room, and the grub swilled down with an excellent little white wine called Quincy. The mule sated.

***

And so to the task of finding a flat. I had set my heart on a romantic attic in an old Norman house, but these turned out to be dank, cold, dark places, unsung artists propped in the corner, solitary and consumptive. Perhaps I am not alone in feeling uncomfortable in the company of estate agents, afraid that you are being smilingly inveigled into buying a pair of shoes that will seriously damage your feet. I became prickly and suspicious, and it was a miracle that in this state of mind I was able to achieve anything. But I did, and remarkably quickly. The little marvel who led me to the Maison de Mule was not the caricature, silver-tongued estate agent, but a young girl just out of business school, stumbling in the street, fumbling with the keys and asking apologetically, 'Ca vous déplait?' as I paced around the flat. But I was far from displeased. It was snug and warm, deeply, soothingly blue, with a view over the whole town. And through a door, source of many a merry ablution, one of those little one step baths that you sit in. I came back the next day just to check the view was still there, paid a 10% deposit, and within 48 hours of starting out, the place was as good as mine.

***

Well I'm currently sitting in the quietest café in a little town called Auffay, which is on the picturesque River Scie that runs between Rouen and Dieppe. Total Hicksville, yet still boasting 101 quality patisseries, charcuteries, fish shop, ironmonger, poodle parlour, butcher and très petite town hall. The little hostelry is wondrously blessed with no piped music, but things did get a little too quiet when this character at the bar began huffing and sighing volubly, and kept this up for a full ten minutes. Half expecting him to cleave open the bar with an axe, when the arrival of a tarte à l'oignon appeared to pacify him, and a sudden influx of people dispelled the sinister air. Two youths pulverising a table football machine, two women who've brought in their own sandwiches, and two more drinking coffee. Positive commotion in here now.

Anyway, when I've finished this jus de raisin I must away back to the big city, because at 4 o'clock the keys to the kingdom are handed over. I am glad I didn't choose a place like this in the country, nightfall extinguishing any flicker of activity. In the absence of writing a symphony the tranquillity would have been unbearable. The legal proceedings took place in the notaire's majestic office, all white and light overlooking the historic town hall. It was too late to get started that day, as there was no power yet in the flat, so I made for the Bistrot Parisienne where an excellent fish terrine, lamb stew and orange flavoured rice pud came to the princely sum of 65 francs[1]. It's a cosy little place, the front half a café bar with conversation and jazz music, partitioned from the restaurant where all things important emanate from a hatch. Knock, knock-out come the dishes. Knock, knock, knock – give me a large beer; the empty glass reappearing just 30 seconds later.

The night proved sleepless as I had no alarm, and

---

[1] Conversion to the euro only happened in 2002, but the franc already feels like a distant relic of history. To get an idea of value, just think 10 francs to the pound.

the hotel would not supply a wake-up call. This last fact rather irksome, as I'd always greatly valued the Hotel Normandya for its unpretentious homely quality – warm, cheap, quiet and not a hint of cable TV. Run by one of those perfectly coiffured, undemonstrably assertive madames who seem to dominate so many bars and pensions. Unfortunately, tonight it was her shadow, the husband, who answered my request for an early wake-up call. Always adorned in an apron, bow tie and scowl, he indicated the impossibility of such a request. So the Mule, who loves an unimpaired sleep, had to listen out to each chime of the church clock, so as not to miss the furniture delivery from England. Tiptoed downstairs at 7.00am, and there he was, salaud shadow, portender of no sleep; very much awake.

I hardly dared believe the furniture would arrive – Force 8 gale, bow doors open. But there was the van beside the house, the driver asleep in his cab. Then came the carpenter, to assess this and that, followed by Mr EDF to turn on the electric, and finally, the concierge to set the waters flowing through the old pipes. Quelle Joie! Since then, been painting, equipping and drinking in that view. The whole of Rouen is spread out below. The hills on the left, the town hall, Cathedral, dungeon, and at one point where no buildings intercede, the Seine. Every skyscape, every time of day lends a different impression, with great industrial chimneys making their own contribution to whatever the natural elements are doing. Just now, the light is fading in a mainly clear, blue sky. A thin bank of cloud above the horizon, contains the reddy brown vapour from a distant chimney, creating a distinctive sunset of its own. Dead ahead, far away, a radio mast semaphors a signal across the night.

***

Rouen is a town divided by the Seine, a wide, working stretch of river that meanders its way upto the sea at Le Havre. One side, the Rive Gauche, is relatively flat and unspectacular, never having recovered from wartime obliteration. It is best explored on the excellent metro system, which wends under and over ground like a gentle fairground ride, before dividing onto grass-laned tracks that take you to the very outskirts of town. The housing estates seem to have a high quotient of nurseries and swimming pools, all named after landmarks of French culture. There is something mildly wonderful about taking the Georges Braque metro on your way to L'école Albert Camus.

The left bank contains one of the most appalling examples of modern architecture, the soaring concrete monolith which houses the city archive, and obscures the view of the cathedral for thousands of people. Presumably the authorities cherish it as a triumph of the New, and refuse to acknowledge its absolute ugliness. A similar blight has appeared on Brighton seafront, a rusting curve of tank track, commissioned by the Council, and bolted onto the beach, foundations stretching 20 feet into the shingle. The greater the folly, the deeper they dig. Our only hope is that the seagulls have their collective beak put out by this monstrosity arisen on their patch, descend in furious flock upon the rusting hulk, and with a mighty squawk, carry it away to some grim sandbank, downwind of a nuclear reactor, where it might sink without trace.

The other side, the Rive Droite, contains the historic architecture and is surrounded by commanding hilltops at Mont Saint Aignan, Bonsecours and Canteleu. All offer wonderful views of Rouen, but probably the most impressive are from Bonsecours. The road up is too steep and car-ridden to attempt on foot, so the best bet is the13 bus from the florist near the station. Just behind the basilisque near Bonsecours village hall, you look down onto the Seine as it wends its way through the countryside from Paris. Turn back through the high street, then along the Rue de la Corniche, and you arrive at a vantage point where you seem to stand on top of the whole town. I got there just before noon on a Sunday morning, and all the churches of Rouen were ringing out, powerfully and haphazardly, finally diminishing to one stray, lolling bell. A steep winding path led down the hillside back to town. Over the railway tracks, up Rue Martainville, and I arrived at the thriving Sunday market in Place Saint Marc where an Armenian oompah band was in full swing.

The best way of discovering the Rive Droite, is simply to take a week meandering around on foot. One of the attractions is the amount of art on display, not just in museums but the many private galleries around town. There is a surprise exhibition of modern art within a bank, near the old market square. You enter through the beautiful, ancient edifice of L'Hôtel de Bourgtheroulde, cross a courtyard of friendly statues, into a hall of huge African carvings and canvases bursting with colour. The streets around L'église Saint Maclou are full of studios for carpentry and sculpture, and the Rue Eau de Robec, a little stream running down one side, has no less than three lutheries making violins, guitars and mandolins. This street features in 'L'Horla', a collection of short stories by Maupassant, and does not seem to have changed much in the intervening years. Rouen is an historic town where the past has been preserved alongside the modern.

***

There are just six days before the ferry conducts its final voyage to Newhaven. What will happen to that drab little army of duty free shoppers who go ashore for just one hour, and trundle into Dieppe with their shopping trolleys to stock up on booze and fags? It would be much more logical if all the duty-free shopping in Britain were located in a huge nicotined hangar in Basildon, and all the shopping trolleys and anodyne conversation could be drawn there, without this perverse need to cross the Channel. On the boat two women produced a flask, and poured the steaming water into their pot noodles. I had never before seen a pot noodle prepared, but they set about the task with such intense purpose, stirring carefully and watching the clock, before judging the time ready to dip in and savour. And then they commented, in quite animated fashion, on the new flavour. Twenty minutes from a town where you can get a three course meal of fish soup, mussels and apple pie for £6.00, these ladies were absorbed in their pot noodle.

Round about the Maison de Mule are some very solid, respectable buildings, all perfectly maintained, with gates, post boxes and chimney pots puffing away in the evening. Some are quite enormous, with majestic drives and gardens, all protected by intercoms and massive iron railings bearing the image of a fearsome Alsatian. There are so many French films set in such surroundings, where papa comes home dutifully from work, the whole family sit round the table… and then gruesome reality breaks through the veneer of contentment.

In the middle of the night, a month or so ago, an enormous row broke out in one of the houses below my window. I have never heard such howling rage, the police were called, and the next morning I fully expected to see signs of blood and broken glass. But in fact normality had already resumed, just one perfectly clothed and coiffured lady, inspecting the mark along her car, before silently driving away. Being a total stranger in this town, I do have the unparalleled opportunity of ignoring the social conventions, and am torn between being existential man and conforming. 'Bonjour madame, quel orage hier soir'. Contributing to the inane tinkle of conversation, so that I might belong.

***

I'm sat in my little, local Algerian eaterie on the Boulevard de la Marne, having polished off a wondrous couscous. Outside was deeply cold, down to the bone marrow, but now the Mule is fed and contented, wind gently popping from both ends. It seems wherever you eat in France, the fodder finished, the waiter will tempt you with 'un petit café, monsieur?' as if defying you to resist something so inconsequential, but also delivered with a frisson conveying there might be more to this beverage than a thimble of black coffee. Anyway, declined the Algerian coffee, knowing that an awesome Italian cuppa awaited me at Brasserie Paul, situated beneath the very walls of the old Cathedral. A tape of Scott Joplin music winds its way round and round, but that has to be better than the piped radio that seems to afflict almost every other public place. In fact, last week I took a little train journey to Elbeuf Saint Aubin, to discover a town that was '1984' with a baguette under the arm. Loud Eurovision song contest music tannoyed through windswept streets, accompanied by manic presenters engaged in ball numbingly banal banter. When I rule Rouen, the first edict will be for nubile youths to besport themselves on the banks of the Seine every morning. The second will be to torch the tannoy.

But of course, to everything there are exceptions, and this morning after doing a few errands, I installed myself in the Café Bovary where there is – no music, just people talking, some loud, some in a whisper, but above all, in peace. Presided over by a lean, softly spoken man, who brings you un grand café crème.

49

Still more quietly old fashioned is the Café Metropole near the station. The central column is thick with posters from the past, 'spectacles', exhibitions, daredevil deeds beneath the Big Top. Nothing in the decor or furnishings makes any concession to modern fashion; it is rather stark but still. The patron walks stiffly in his polished, crisp shoes, silver haired, waterey eyed, exuding a sense of time and dignity.

It seems the owners of each flat form a sort of co-operative to organise the maintenance of the house, and tomorrow is the annual meeting. I read the voluminous minutes of the last one, and was alarmed at mention of asbestos. Pencilled an iron lung operation into my diary. Well the meeting was quite an event. Ten owners rent their flats, with just two resident, the Mule and an embittered hag whose role it is to uphold the moral fibre of the house against collective assault from prostitution, drugs and partying. With each invective against the forces of darkness her voice became more shrill and strident, as if to fend off the animosity ranged against her, evidently established over many years, and which occasionally burst through the protocol of politeness in expressions of ridicule and contempt. At the meetings' end, no one proferred the obligatory handshake, and she descended the little spiral staircase into her own private hell. Imagine my alarm the next morning, when she cornered me in the street and was effusively friendly, insistent on the need to surveil all that goes on in the house, and offering to show me her photos taken from Mont Saint Aignan. Book me in for that operation. A trolley in the corridor will do just fine.

***

Toilets have undergone a transformation in France. I remember on a school trip in the late sixties, recourse to a public facility was to be avoided at all costs. No semblance of a seat, just two stark footsteps raised above the abyss. A rusty nail on the wall with a few shards of newspaper; on desperate occasions you looked up to discover the nail starkly bare. And the flushing mechanism was a lottery. Either totally redundant, leaving the malarial swamp unmoved, or geared to unleash such a torrent of water, you had to spring from the starting blocks to avoid an unsolicited anal irrigation.

Today, as if by national decree, these cubicles have been transformed into places of sanitary splendour. Softly lit, luxuriously tiled, abundant hot water and then copious folds of crisp linen towelling to end ones' ablution. Just occasionally you step into the recesses of a café and encounter something from the past. Such was the experience in Vernon, a town midway between Rouen and Paris. I had just been served the most execrable cup of coffee. The bar boasted a gleaming espresso machine, but this cup had been drawn from a bottle of camp coffee dating back to pre-war times. Eager to purge myself of the foul essence, I sought out the facility, and there in yellow-tinged sepia, was the urinal, bizarrely shrouded behind a shower curtain. It was as if gliding down the aisle on a modern TGV train, you slide open the compartment door to discover an old third class carriage with joltingly bonehard benches, black clad peasant women and a plump-faced girl clutching a hen.

Vernon is a pleasant little town sloping down to the banks of the Seine, where there is an open air swimming pool and castles either side of the bridge. Turn right and Giverny, home of Monets' garden, is just an hours' walk away. The river road is rather busy, but you can cut upto a cycle path which is altogether more peaceful. One of the joys of being in Normandy is discovering it as the home of impressionist art. Every little civic gallery boasts, Renoir, Sisely, Pissaro et al. The sky hung low and threatening, and I hurried on to avoid the deluge and in anticipation of the little hump-back bridge, those water lilies.

Giverny was totally deserted, just one shop open and a war cemetery. It transpired that Monets' garden was closed until Easter. I tried scaling the walls to get a glimpse of dappled colours reflected in the pond, but they were built to deter intruders, and I traipesed away disconsolate. Oh well, at least the rain had held off, and probably it was all sanitised memorabilia within the fortress. I lifted my head, and there was a little sheltered field with ostriches bounding among sheep and goats. I hadn't seen an ostrich since that episode of 'Northern Exposure' when Maurice, the retired astronaut, tried to persuade Marilyn to sell her ostrich eggs as part of a sure-fire money spinner. The little, round indian quietly mused before deciding to leave those ostrich eggs with their long-legged mummy. Denied Monet, but glad to re-discover Marilyn.

***

Last trip of the winter, and then it's back to open the arch beneath the prom. At the terminal check in at Portsmouth (and isn't terminal an appropriate word for these ante-rooms to hell) 'Tracey, how can I help you' was having problems with her computer, and had to splay herself under the desk to try and rectify matters. She was down there so long, I half suspected she had snuffed it, her spirit E-mailing away to that great website in the sky. But she re-emerged manfully, blue uniform askew, red in the face, cursing the new technology.

On board, implausibly, some lively quavers were floating through the air. I descended the staircase to discover three hikers giving forth on guitar and bongos, only for a French, blue-clad Tracey to appear, daughter of Stalin, and instruct them to cease immediately, as any improptu display of music would result in the ship sinking with all hands in a sea of vipers. To my shame, I said nothing, and nauseous, air-conditioned normality was restored.

Last night I was in this packed café, where a weekly philosophical debate takes place, this time, that old chestnut 'Does free will exist?' The master of ceremonies, a University lecturer, clasped his brow, laughed inappropriately, social skills somewhat dislocated. The microphone circulated, providing one intense contribution after another, a few indulgent

53

intellos reluctant to relinquish the phallic form. I drifted home, mind wandering to the Mrs.Merton show, when the little lady would spring up and announce 'Let's all have a big debate. Norman, why did Bet Lynch leave the Street?' I awoke from this reverie to the sound of the doorbell, an official calling to include me in the French census. So I completed the form, half Norman half Mule, for that is indeed my new heritage. Not a part of the day goes by without me thinking of Mr. Billy Mule. This morning, in the little park opposite La Musée des Beaux Arts, there were two little puppies gamboling around. And he was a pup really, endearing and not yet tamed. Once I was doing some writing, and he was cooking a surprisingly tasty rice dish. He scuttled under the desk and put his chin on my knee. Or he would stretch out on the sofa and stroke his neck on the arm piece like a sleepy hound. We were going to get a dog when he was released. And a goat. Well that is all long ago, but the memories remain.

Chapter 2

Of wars and waterways

For six summers I have looked out of the café onto three bands of colour; beach, sea and sky. Bands of change. Overcast pebbles darken grey and beige, brighten to warm hues of orange, and glisten as new when evening rains clear beneath a slanting sun. One day the sea can surge powerfully, brown and muddy, threatening to engulf us all. The next, Brighton Mediterannean. Shimmering splendour beneath a clear, blue sky, the gulls floating serenely on a big, big pond. A steamy haze fusing the horizon, the heat dense and palpable as the fish are turned on the charcoal grill. To the left, the view is bordered by the Palace Pier, its air thick with fat fryers, gaming machines and the fairground beat of pop music. To the right the West Pier, broken but majestic, somehow still standing. The sun nestles down behind it as a huge flock of birds gather up the darkness and alight upon their derelict home. Then the sky turns a deep, soothing blue before succumbing to the night.

Within this tableau a cast of thousands. Fractious families, pirouetting queens, roller boarding skating teens, troupes of girls on an all day hen night, London lads out for the crack, film crews, joggers, bongo wongo drummers and old age pensioners in Ena

Sharples mac. Being Brighton, the crazy quotient is high. One wet and thankless day, the café desolate, a legless wonder floated in on a skateboard and ordered a mushroom omelette and banana bread, which he ate off a chair, while maintaining a seafaring monologue in impenetrable Geordie. Then there's the dyslexic street dancer who passes by each evening, always with a gentle surprise in store. A granny shopping trolley stuffed with pink grapefruit, a new tutu or a beautifully innocent insight into life. And each dawn, a straggling chorus line of beachcombers, meticulously waving their minesweepers over the stones.

This season has wound its way round, ending with a bang and a whimper. A heatwave lasting well into September, cut dead by weeks of torrential rain. This deluge was clearly the sign to shut up shop and return to Rouen. The cavalry had come in the form of Hoverspeed, restoring the Channel link with a nippy, little ferry that bounces across in just two hours. Some trains arrive inauspiciosly at the butt end of a town, but Rouen station is different. A majestic entrance hall leads out onto a cascade of water and a wide avenue that takes you right into the heart of things. I strode down past the Café Metropole, retracing my old footsteps, hungry to reclaim ownership of the town. It was strange to see the city in leaf for the first time, end of the line leaf, but still an improvement on the bare, black branches which is all I had known before. Gardens still sporting roses and abundant chrysanthemums, and the huge trees in front of the Musée des Beaux Arts, resplendent in their foliage.

Little seems to have changed. The restoration of the Cathedral has progressed, with less scaffolding revealing more pristine stone and delicate design. Then absolute shock. The Café de la Grande Poste is no more, totally gutted in preperation to re-appear as a bank. I walked through town in the soft drizzle, looking for reassuring signs of familiarity. The weekend market was in full swing at the Place Saint Marc. Whole chickens and legs of pork turning on giant spits. Huge saucer-shaped vats cooking spicy rice with king prawns, ratatouille and sauerkraut with jumbo sausages. Trays of pigs trotters set in their jelly, fresh walnuts, marinated prunes, wild mushrooms, gleaming fish and rounds of local cheeses. I bought a cheese set with walnuts, three artichokes, a dozen langoustines and a lettuce that seemed positively alive.

Headed off towards the artists quarter near St. Maclou and looked round the gallery 'Racines du Ciel'. Wandered up a nearby passage, and there was the most beautiful Norman courtyard, with some of the timbers painted a beguiling baby blue. Went down the next alleyway to find a large, verdant square of low timbered buildings, the home of L'école des Beaux Arts. That's the beauty of Rouen; you can be in quite familiar territory, turn around and discover some completely new little corner of contentment. Be warned though, as you crane and marvel at the roofs and spires, take time to look down because Rouen is dog turd city. The town hall, which otherwise excels in the cleaning department, is determined to deal with the problem. They have painted white dachshund logos on the pavement, with an arrow beneath, pointing directly to the gutter. The dogs of Rouen can no longer be in any doubt as to their civic responsibility. Yet they remain stubbornly undeterred. I have written to Monsieur le Maire, advising that he turn his attention from the canines to those impeccably dressed ladies who lead them on. The devil, Monsieur, lies in the stiletto.

***

After days of drizzle, dawn broke with a clear, blue sky, pale and tenuous at first, but growing in confidence as the sun rose. On such a morning it seemed right to give Giverny a second try, and see Monets' garden in its autumn clothes. I hired a bicycle outside Vernon station, crossed the Seine and pedalled carefree through the soft sunshine. I was half expecting a repeat of 'Monet in the Twentieth Century', at Londons' Royal Academy, where the crowds were so great, you ended up feeling like a cow tetchily swishing a tail at the flies in front of its face. In fact, the tide of tourism had pulled out, and the gardens were maintained in a state of casual splendour, making for a great sense of tranquility. It seemed as if every flower and border were in full bloom, producing one last crescendo of colour before the gates were shut, November took hold and the fairies departed the water lily pond.

Giverny was very quiet, and I sat down for lunch at 'La Terrasse', a tiny café with just four tables. The kindly owner prided herself on only using local produce; cheeses, charcuterie, cider, honey bread and ice creams. The charcuterie platter was excellent, especially an orange-scented duck terrine. A glass of local apple juice simply irrigated the tongue and tarte normande was a perfect combination of soft fruit and crisp pastry. What a rich heritage. Cycling along I had passed a little shop selling honey from a local beekeeper, and signs for 'artisan cuisinier et traiteur'. Even the little lane from Vernonnet was named after André Touftel, a master baker who had served his community for fifty four years. Yet leafing through the daily paper 'Libération', I came across a news item about chefs marching on the National Assembly, protesting at a VAT regime that favours takeaway foods, and proclaiming 'la mort de la cuisine traditionelle'. Time will tell, but France seems well adept at fostering the old alongside the new. Elsewhere in the paper was an article by the Guadaloupe writer Maryse Condé, part of a series considering the world as it enters the new millennium. 'Ò Do not listen to sorrowful spirits and above all do not fear for the uniqueness of the region to which you belong. The culture of a people never dies. It is a living matter which changes in order to adapt itself to new needs.'

On the way back I visited Vernon museum, which is a beautiful old building with one very light and modern gallery attached. You follow through a series of rooms, ending among the rafters with 'Les artistes de Giverny'. There are some pretty big names here, including Pierre Bonnard and members of the Monet family. Further downstairs, the exhibits on local history reveal a litany of disasters. 1870, invasion by Prussia, and total destruction of the bridge across the Seine. 1914, a tide of Belgian refugees and blank exhaustion in the faces of the 'poilus' returning from the front. 1940, massive bombardment of the town, followed by further destruction of the bridge as the Germans fought a fierce rearguard action. The sword and scabbard of an English officer killed in this battle is displayed in a glass case; a modern war fought with almost medieval intensity.

Intrigued by the local impact of war, I went to Clères, a village about twenty miles north of Rouen, to visit the Museum of the 1944 Liberation. Unfortunately it was all shut up. The owner had recently died and his sons sold off the exhibits to pay what was owed. Only a rusty mortar gun was left, sitting on a bank. Just along from the old museum is the Parc Zoologique de Clères. A path shaded by huge trees wends its way round richly green lawns and a magnificent château. A sequence of wonderful birds pass by, some confined but most free to wander beside you. Peacocks, black swans and ducks nestling a beak on their backs. A cluster of pink flamingos perched still and serene in the shallows. Gently the path rises uphill, and you're walking above the lake, the sun filtering orange and green through the leaves, little deer nosing a soft-eyed interest.

You come down behind the château at an immaculate Norman house, with lightly mauve timbers, lattice windows and clematis reddening on the walls. Through a gate there's an old ruin, totally colonised by trees and shrubs, just a single arch rising intact above its new habitation. In the grounds of the château, three most wonderful birds, a sort of black and white peacock with red cheeks, electric eyes and vibrant beige crown shining in the sun. Why leave this enclave of tranquility? Take another turn, there are few restrictions here. No stern little white-chained fences keeping you from where you want to be. I glided round again, and sat quietly in the sun on a stone bench, the birds occasionally squawking, the clock tower sounding the hour.

Finally I left the park, and noticed a monument directly opposite, dedicated to the village war dead. Twenty nine dead in the first world war and eight in the second, of which five were shot as 'victimes civiles'. On the walls of the station waiting room are plaques to three railway workers killed during the German occupation. The park and the monument, the bridge and Giverny. Symbols of war and peace in such close proximity. Sanctuaries so tranquil they might have eased the mayhem of shellshocked minds.

***

Down to the reference library in search of a little local knowledge. The stone staircase divides and sweeps up two storeys, the walls adorned with old prints of the town, and a large canvas of learned scholars with thinking caps and quill pens. The main reference area is vast and open plan with wide, spacious desks. From where I am sitting you can watch out across the rooftops, to the towers of the Abbaye Saint Ouen. A smaller room, reserved for ancient texts, looks down onto three Raoul Dufy murals in the museum next door. Books are chronicled on cards in long, wooden draws; there is not a microfiche catalogue in sight. You fill in a book request and wait for a librarian to bring it to your desk. Gazing around, most of the readers look like students or academics, but there is an assortment of other people presumably brought in by the sense of sanctuary. To my left, a woman rhythmically turning the pages of an old journal, a look of gentle wonderment on her face. A baglady in oversized shoes shuffles through to join her and also settles to a journal, a commotion of panting and pullovers swiftly consumed by the silence.

My mind wanders to l'Abbaye Saint Ouen which in any other town would take centre stage, but here plays second fiddle to the cathedral. Its walls blackened, ornamental finesse in tatters, the interior always colder than the outside world. High up, defying the gloom, sparklingly colourful windows provide the pearl in this street urchins' pocket. They are calling closing time for lunch, there is a packing of bags and the cohort descends the stairs. In the entrance hall, partly obscured by a partition stand, I notice a memorial to the thirty two Normandy writers killed in the first world war. It was inaugurated on the 11th of November 1939, the twentieth anniversary of 'la grande victoire'.

***

On the Rive Droite, much of what lies West of the

Boulevard des Belges is given over to traffic and cut price warehouses. No one is intended to negotiate this area on foot, so I got on a Number 2 bus for Conforama, in search of a plank of wood. You may recall some years ago, a trilogy of French films entitled 'Three colours: Red, White and Blue'. A memorable image is repeated of a tiny, decrepid woman, stretching painfully to push a bottle through the opening of a recycling bank. I've always wondered whether they captured this spontaneously on film, or whether the scene was actually rehearsed. Well mystery solved. As the bus ground to a halt, I saw the very crone conducting a repeat performance at a pillar box. Having finally succeeded in posting the letter, she turned back, anxious eyes resting upon the chasm of life. Had the letter dropped? Was it stamped? Would they ever reply? There is only so much pain you can take in a traffic jam. Thankfully the bus pulled away.

The main redeeming feature of this neighbourhood is the Préfecture de la Région de Haute Normandie. Much of the old architecture in Rouen is a bit the worse for wear, angels who've lost their heads, masonry corroded or blackened with time. The Prefecture, though, is immaculate in its splendour. Four huge and perfectly gilded pillars flank the entrance, lined by immense buildings of châteauesque proportions. Impeccably uniformed police patrol the perimeter. This is merely the seat of local government, but there are presidents of nation states who would give their eye teeth for the power that emanates from the Prefecture.

Just around the corner is the Flaubert museum, birthplace of the author of 'Madame Bovary'. You step through into a secluded garden, ring the bell and wait to be ushered in. The exhibits are as much about papa and brother Flaubert, who pioneered surgical advance in the region, as they are about the writer himself. There are showcases of instruments involving multiple springs and levers, anatomical waxworks and a grotesque soft doll designed to demonstrate the process of childbirth. In a grand salon overlooking the prefecture, an antique dentists' chair sits alongside a pedal-driven drill. Portraits look down revealing the physicians to be quite fastidious in their dress sense. In one picture involving a manual excavation up an anus, the surgeon is dressed in full waistcoat, jacket and knee-length leather boots. Four immaculately attired staff look on impassively as the poor patient quivers in agony. Somehow this image lingers longer in the mind than the rather tame showcase containing the authors' famous stuffed parrots.

Just about six miles further along the Rive Droite the house that Gustave Flaubert moved to, at Croisset on the Côte de Canteleu. The next day, bright and blue, I hired a bike and cycled down there. The bank of the Rive Droite is pretty inaccessible due to the swathe of road and railway that runs above it. An attempt has been made to pedestrianise a short stretch of boulevard, but until the saplings grow, there is nothing between you and the traffic. Just a few working barges are moored alongside, a far cry from the days of 'L'Atlante', the classic black and white movie following a pre-war barge journey from Paris to Le Havre. The boulevard gives way to deserted store houses, lorry parks and disused railway tracks, the sort of desolate urban landscape scripted for gangland feuds and mental anguish. The padre and Marlon Brando on the Waterfront. Roquentin stalking across wasteland in Sartres' 'Nausea'. And any settling of debts involving the Corleone family. Up ahead Canteleu is perched on a hilltop, great blocks of high-rise housing making a powerful pattern against the sky. On the opposite bank, huge cranes manoeuvre the cargo from foreign ships into flour mills. At one point you can take a little ferry across to Grand Quévilly, and wander among vast gasometers, scrapyards and chemical complexes. The source of many a smouldering sunset in Rouen.

The bank at Croisset is much more tranquil, with picturesque houses set against a white chalk escarpment. Gustave Flauberts' house has actually been knocked down, and all that remains is a dinky little 'pavillon' with an old school bell and a garden of pleasant shade. The author is said to have paced beneath the lime trees, talking his thoughts out loud, only committing a line to paper when it actually sounded right. Inside the pavillon are several of his artefacts; his desk, a goose quill pen, a clay pipe and another stuffed parrot. Just a few hundred yards along, lunch can be had for as little as forty francs in a Norman barn called 'Le Pulqué'. The tables are pleasantly set out, and across one wall stretches a bright, modern mural with smiling faces, big eyes and spiky hair, a sort of hippy punk version of the Bayeux tapestry. In a far corner, dimly lit, tables bare, the novelty of a non-smoking area, which can only ever have been used for fast days or the laying out of a coffin. For in France, smoking is obligatory in public places; 'Je fume, donc je suis.' Your host and chef is a genial character of Robbie Coltrane proportions, who wraps an enormous apron round his midriff when food is ordered, and manages to keep up a healthy banter while sautéing coquilles Saint Jacques in the kitchen. Robbie, in truth Gerard, has been here for twenty five years, retreating from the hothouse kitchens of Boulevard Hausmann in Paris, to seek a quieter life. He has always meant to change the name on the sign, but in a country as regulatory as France, that would involve twelve months of paperwork, so Le Pulqué has stuck; a quintesentially French restaurant named after a punchy Mexican cactus drink. The scallops by the way, were superb, cooked with wild mushrooms and a little cognac, and not too heavy for the bike ride ahead.

I slowly climbed a long, steep road through the woods, eventually arriving on top of Canteleu. Here, there are any number of forest paths to explore, and an arboretum to visit. In one enclosure lives a family of wild boer, the little ones nipping each other in unceremonious fashion. It is reassuring that these snout-faced snappers are kept behind two lengths of wire fencing, as a baby wild boer could do terminal damage to your calf muscles. Undeterred by smoking wheels of rubber. Across the way, in a sunnier aspect, three goats of the multiple horned variety. To a London boy, any untethered beast is replete with menace, so I pedalled on through the forest, letting the shafts of sunlight and swirling treetops sweep the animal out of my mind.

Heading back to Rouen, a cold East wind had picked up, and after an unparalleled eight days of unbroken sunshine, the city returned to its familiar coating of mist and cloud. Quite exhausted back at the boulevard, it was indeed a wonder to discover a cylindrical glass lift, that took me and the bike upto the bridge where the metro trains trundle across the Seine. From there it was just a short stretch to the south wall of the Cathedral and 'Thé Majiscule', a café of paintings, second hand books and seriously comforting cakes.

***

Down to Newhaven with my own trusty bike, and there was a frisson of agitation around the terminal building. The hostess in the purple bowler hat was trying valiantly to assuage people who had risen early and travelled down to discover an empty jetty and an empty day. Stormy weather over the French coast and all hope of a crossing abandoned. The crowd lingered, suspended in time, eventually returning home to pick up the dog and the note for the milkman. The next day the winds abated, the sea was calm and the Italian captain predicted a pleasant journey; something of a rarity for this little hovercraft that even manages to bobble about within the harbour walls. The captain has become a fond presence over the intercom, with his Chico Marx diction and advice to lash down small children when venturing out onto the sundeck. Unfortunately the sundeck fails to provide those exhilarating lungfuls of sea air, managing instead to capture the full complement of black vapour streaming from the ships' funnels. Undeterred, the passengers slip into ancient mariner mode, adjusting their headgear in trusted seafaring fashion, gamely attempting to light a pipe, striding purposefully across decks to grasp their very own stretch of boat rail and look deeply out to sea.

First out of the hatch when the boat docked, cycling free as a bird. Woolfed down a gigot d'agneau at the Café de l'Union, booked up a room for next weeks herring festival and still had ten minutes to spare before the 12.59 tootled off to Rouen. For a cyclist, the Rue Jeanne d'Arc is blissfully free of traffic on a Sunday, but the cobblestones inflict all manner of mischief on the old backbone. I decided to make for Dieppedale, a little village beyond Croisset which runs between the river and the chalk cliff. Within the cliff itself is a champignonerie, a series of dark, dank grottoes where mushrooms are cultivated in huge sacks of horse manure. The tour begins with a tasting of the local rhubarb nectar, and then you're off beneath the cliff, only the guides' flickering lamp and the centuries old ceiling coming between you and total oblivion. The guide is a great believer in interactive learning. 'Smell that horse manure'; general chorus of approval. 'Smell the spores of the mycellum'. Again an almost intoxicant inhalation. 'Feel the weight of that mushroom'; my what a colossus, bring me a forklift. Anyway, not a place to linger too long, as the moisture pervades your every layer of clothing in an insidious and dispiriting fashion. Architecture of the ultimate dungeon. It seems the caves were excavated by prisoners in the 14th and 15th centuries, and the stones shipped onto barges for the construction of the cathedral.

Back at the mouth of the grotto the warmth factor was nil and I felt the need of a restorative couscous. There are certain magical dishes in cuisine which you imagine have bubbled away since the beginning of time, the pot ever replenished, the liquor a lustrous golden brown. On the Normandy coast it's a soup de poisson, in Marseilles a bouillabaisse, chez Yaya and Hassina, the sauce for their couscous. The grain, dusted with cinnamon, soaks up the ancient flavours, the vegetables are meltingly tender and the portions enormous. It's always an effort getting your legs from under the table and out the door. You smile like a simpleton and nod contentedly as Hassina raises a curly spouted teapot high into the air, and pours seamlessly into an ornamental little cup. Eventually ambulant again, it's a shock to step outside and encounter a marathon run in full flood, the front cohorts striding by like stallions, the later ranks willing but disoriented, the final straggler, bandana askew, bravely raising his hooves high in the air but making little progress in a forward direction. Behind him a lone steward with an outstetched orange flag, holds back an enormous pile of French traffic. Foot pedals itching for the kill.

***

One summer night in Dieppe, an African dance band attracted a huge crowd, set off across the lawns between the castle walls and the port, mounted a stage and amid a rising crescendo of drumbeats, orchestrated the most spectacular firework display I have ever seen. There has been such a buzz of expectation around the Dieppe herring festival, I assumed it must deliver the same degree of entertainment with the added bonus of freshly cooked fish. Well there is certainly plenty of fish about. Herrings and scallops are barbecued outside every café in town, though not in a particularly celebratory manner. The herrings produce great wafts of smoke, and the food comes served in plastic plates with wine in a plastic cup. Hundreds of second hand stalls line the streets near the entrance to the dock, with everything you would never wish to buy. Top of the pile on one stall, a hospital issue urine bottle. Where was the show of festivity? No flame-eating monocyclist in fancy dress, no live music, not even a mime artist caught in a glass cage. The only entertainment on offer was a ferocious spat between two fishwives as they circled a water pump, backs arched, tails beating against the ground. It was all over in the space of a firecracker, then the chestnut seller and the little fairground ride put their things away and by nine o'clock the revelry was at an end.

Most of the bars were pretty desolate, loud TV sport filling the void, but I did find a cosy piano bar near the rising bridge, with decent music and original oil paintings, one of a madame stretching across her chaise longue, laceing up her long leather boots. The prices were exorbitant though, and I returned to the Pension where too much unspent energy denied the onset of sleep. The bed produced the knack of unmaking itself, and with the reading light on, a fat old fly revved into life, banging off the walls, stubbornly refusing to exit the wide-opened windows. Any last vestiges of heat had now flown the crumpled nest, and simultaneous messages started lighting up indicating empty belly and bladder full. There was not a scrap of food to be had and the toilet down the corridor had a dangerously dodgy door handle. When needs must, the Mule has been known to produce liberating arcs of sparklement from improbable places, most notably the top of Nelsons' tower in Edinburgh, but here all windows looked out onto a common courtyard, and at this moment in the 'mad cow' trade war it seemed impolitic to unleash a torrential pounding onto the cobblestones below. Eons of time passed by before I eventually got up, shod, shuffled down the corridor and availed myself of the facility. Door firmly ajar.

Awoke with the upper quadrant of my body totally paralysed. My neck had been stretched across that hideous log which in France masquerades as a pillow, severing all supplies of blood and the like. How can you enjoy a nights' sleep snuggled upto something with all the comfort of a cosh? That's me finished for the weekend, I'm off for the early train. By all means visit Dieppe for the wonderful view from the castle walls, and the tumbledown churches with their gulls and gargoyles. But if you're feeling

71

festive around the second weekend in November, then stay away because believe me, herrings are made for health not happiness. I creaked down the stairs, unbolted the door and walked into the rain, waiting for the first café to show signs of life.

It's always beguiling watching a skilled waiter in action. One hand holds the laden tray aloft, while the other opens bottles, pours, wipes and dispenses change. Orders are usually called out to the bar, but this early in the morning the waiter had to perform a lone tour de force, greeting customers, making coffee, pulling glasses of 'pression' and passing comment on the cold. Eventually la Patronne swanned in, took up residence at the bar, scraped her high heels round a bit and looked distractedly down her fingernails. The warmth and hubub in the café almost enticed me to stay, but the harm had been done and I saddled up and away.

Given an unexpectedly free day, I decided to head for Le Havre. Cognissenti may think this a strange choice, as Le Havre is a bleak town, raised totally during the bombing raids of 1944, and reborn a perfect example of planners blight. The streets are flat regimented wind tunnels, the only distinctive feature being a little funicular railway that scales the hillside. For just two francs a go, it fills up with prams, bicycles and in my compartment a row of three old ladies, grimly wrapped against the cold. The town looks no more inspiring from above, but the setting of sea and sky is magnificent, and the narrow stairways and passages back down are fun. Anyway, I had really come to visit the Museé André Malraux, a modern building between the docks and the port de plaisance. Once inside there is a wonderful feeling of light and space. A mezzanine contains the intricate detail of early portraiture, and down below the local painters famous for impressionism and fauvism. The deep blues of Raoul Dufy seem to melt into your mind, and from a gently sloping walkway you can take in two Monets at a distance, one of the water lilies and a view from Westminster Bridge. The number of exhibits is not overwhelming and you step outside feeling lighter than when you arrived.

The museums in Rouen are also in their different ways, quite captivating; once round you are always reluctant to leave. Historic settings, exhibits charmingly displayed, the information instructive without being too demanding. Visit the dungeon and you pass through the vast fortress that once defended the town, the wars between English and French kings and the imprisonment of Joan of Arc. A short walk downhill, just opposite the library, is the Musée Le Secq des Tournelles containing everything forged from iron and steel over the past thousand years. Daggers, arrowheads and antique guns; candlabras and candle snuffers; hanging pendants, shop signs and balustrades, all the hardware of the narrow cobbled streets. Down one such street, the nearby Rue de l'école, a young woman in her workshop stretches lengths of leather to refurbish worn out book covers and antique tabletops. The craft heritage of Normandy, in safe hands.

***

Today I crossed the border into Picardy. Through the train window, a fine rain sweeps down drenching the countryside. It reminds me of the Bernanos book, 'Journal d'un curé de campagne', about a poor, young Norman priest, constantly trudging through mud and rain, unloved by the local peasantry and finally defrocked by unwitting association with the local gay. L'école Georges Bernanos, just up from me on the Rue de Lille, is built in the image of this book. Thick, unforgiving walls, a huge tolling bell, hard to imagine a shaft of joy infiltrating the classroom. The train pulls into Amiens and the first sight is this solitary, brickwork tower of flats, telescoping into an obelisk. Then strolling around, you discover fine old buildings among the new, a lone turret of a church tower set beside a working crane, a belfry given over to a cycle shop. And then the cathedral, not quite as powerful as Rouen, but still right up there in the premier league of European architecture. The front entrance has just been immaculately restored with rows of wise faces looking down, and inside spectacular stained glass windows, Raoul Dufy blue. Little wonder that in a nearby street, the one form of craft I have not yet seen in Rouen, a master 'vitrailleur', practitioner of art and coloured glass. Down the slope from the cathedral, the modern University is spread out in pleasant fashion with little waterways running here and there. And then you're upon the Somme, such an insignificant stretch of river to have fought over; dark, muddy, sluggish, a surface sheen of petrol. On the far bank, a freshly landscaped park combines trees and water, but however I tried to compose a photograph, horrific images came to mind of a red river, sinking hands, and that plaque within the cathedral walls in homage to Maréchal Foch.

Back across town to the city Museum, where the bare, basement arches contain excavations from the beginnings of time. It seems that Amiens was a key town in the first century A.D., bigger than Paris, commanding the Somme and strategically linking Lyons with Boulogne and London. Much of the permanent exhibition is given over to old religous imagery, before suddenly ending in a room of modern art. Perhaps most impressive is the colour and design of the building itself, with a grand staircase containing tremendous frescos depicting 'work', 'rest' and 'homeland'. There is also a vast white room full of statues, the last an enormous figure of a woman reflecting on old age. Next door, equally impressive, is the city library. Ten pillars of Athenean proportions line the entrance, and inside modern technology and symbols of heritage combine to great effect. Students must be inspired by simply being there.

Walking around Amiens, the cafés seem particularly attractive. In Rouen there are many cafés I feel completely at home in, but others are in truth, totally unappealing. Crummy old furniture, nicotined decor, a bar sparsely peopled and po-faced, life as a glass of pastis eternally eked out with tap water. Perhaps it is the novelty, but in Amiens the cafés seem comforting and distinctive. The 'Lucillus Bar' near the Circus is like an old fashioned inn with low ceilings, wood panelling and a table devoted to serious dice throwing and cigar chomping. Down towards the river is 'Bissap' an African café with lively music and livelier cocktails. I somehow contrived to miss the last train home, and booked into the Victor Hugo, an excellent one star hotel providing warmth, tranquility and perfectly soft pillows.

Invoking the memory of that Bernanos book was not a good idea. Incessant rain ever since, the gargoyles gasping for air. I've travelled South to Evreux capital of the Eure district of Normandy. It's best to time your arrival for lunch because the restaurant opposite the station offers excellent value and a terrific view of the town below. A parkway of tall trees and tumbling water takes you down the hillside to the museum. The basement is built on the ruins of an old Roman settlement, and you rise up through the centuries along a wide, stone spiral staircase. All for free. The nearby cathedral, with its own little moat, is darkly gothic, barely a shaft of light piercing the gloom. Half a mile along is the civic centre, and you have to hand it to the French, they maintain their heritage in style as well as producing terrific new public works. A belfry overlooks the grand town hall, foursquare beside a beautiful old theatre, an Art House and the magnificent town library. The front of the library is about 150 years old and served as a base for the wartime Resistance. This connects with a modern building, one side brick, metal and glass, the roof sloping like the crest of a great wave over the other half, designed like the hulk of an old sailing vessel. In England you become used to libraries and classrooms being housed in portakabins. Things are far from perfect here, in fact a trade union demo has just gone by protesting at local redundancies. But when it comes to civic pride the French are generous and ambitious. Best of all, much of Evreux's splendour can be appreciated from the excellent Café des Arts, windows carefully etched with flowers, the walls and soundtrack carrying images of ragtime and the big band era.

A brook lined with willows takes you back to the hillside park, and on the bus journey home I decided to stop off at Louviers, a small town between Evreux and Rouen. Textile mills once dominated life here, and tributaries of the River Eure run through the town. There are little bridges, locks and an ancient building that now serves as the Conservatoire for musical talent. Some houses have verandas stretching right over the water, perilously close to being inundated. There is a church dating back to the fourteenth century, and around it a series of cobbled streets with small houses built in the old Norman style. The town hall is lit by candlabras and has a little park with a sort of bandstand made out of treetrunks. On the way back to the bustop is the restaurant 'Le jardin des bigards', The Garden of Seville oranges. Inside are soft, comfortable chairs and plants stretching upto the ceiling. More important, the food is good, the place was packed just twenty minutes after opening. I had my first ever 'boudin blanc' a tender white sausage alongside apples and braised potatoes. For pud, a clafoutis or pancake batter, of pears served with homemade custard and chocolate sauce. A contented trail of zzz's escaped the bus back home.

The next day the rains cleared long enough to make a dash for the market at Place Saint Marc. Organics are starting to make an impression with stalls of wholemeal bread and fromage 'biologique'. I bought a jar of acacia honey and explained that my friend Angie had suffered in her bee keeping, due to a disease afflicting the English bees. The stallholder, Monsieur Miel, had heard of bees being driven mad by chemical fertilizers. Perhaps that explains why Angie would hoot hysterically, shriek in my earhole and deliver a stinging thwack to the shoulder as we made pastry at 'The Nosebag' in Oxford. A whirlwind experience, I was eventually sacked for chasing her round the kitchen with a ham bone. Angie would love this market, the little farmers from the 'bocage' down with their few bits of produce. One old lady just has a basket of eggs, two pumpkins and a big tub of thick cream. Another, home-pressed apple juice. And a man offers slices of his enormous juicy pears; one pear a meal in itself.

I made my way upto the Algerian café for Sunday couscous. At the next table a lady has just finished her meal, but lingers for a coffee, a tea and then a decaf. Perhaps she tarries for a purpose, because finally Sharif arrives, a regular customer with slim cigars and the crisp diction that makes his French easy to understand. Would it put her out if he joined her? She feigned insouciance but her face was all animated delight. Every topic of conversation brought forth bursts of laughter; Glenfiddich whisky, the weather even Bournemouth. I went upto the bar and an old Algerian engaged me in conversation. As a twenty year old he had been involved in the Normandy landings. Ten days of hunger and exhaustion before being ordered to advance. As he recounted the tale, phrases kept recurring, 'c'était pas un cadeau', 'cauchemar', 'massacre'. It was as if the words just punctuated a sea of images crossing his mind, bringing tears tumbling down his face. Other countries took prisoners, but not the Germans. Massacre. And had he stayed in Normandy ever since? An absurd laugh. No, after two years he was sent back to Algeria to work as a baker.

***

France is a great country for regulations. Today I passed a sign on a concrete abberation near the Cathedral, forbidding fly posting. Posters could only improve this grey, featureless thoroughfare, but the law of 29th July 1881 had been invoked as an awesome deterrent. A more recent edict, 25th May 1998, is displayed in the premises of master baker Jean-Marie Viard who produces twenty five different types of loaf each day on the Allée Eugene Delacroix. Under this law, no one may use the title 'boulanger' unless they make the dough, then prove and bake it on the premises. It reflects a running battle between the traditional craft and a growing number of drive-in bread shops based on frozen, factory-made products. Taste Maitre Viards' freshly baked 'pain aux abricots et raisins', or his richly walnut 'pain noisette' and you will be sure to return. In Dieppe, the master chocolatier Roussel has a sign protesting at the European regulation which allows British confectionery, based on dairy fats and sugar, to carry the label 'milk chocolate'. In his shop, Maitre Roussel heaves at a huge tub of warm chocolate, working to achieve the perfect sheen. On the wall, a picture of him lovingly smelling a sack full of cocoa beans in their sunny country of origin.

My favourite wall sign is printed at the top of the little path into town, 'Ne pas uriner sur le mur s'il vous plait. Danger.' In some eyes the absence of any legal justification might render the sign redundant, but that final prohibition demands your attention. Logically, you know the only danger can be too hasty a 'fermeture' of the flies, but the seed of doubt has been sown. Danger, a dark alleyway, a porte cullis primed to unleash the Hound of the Baskervilles at the first sniff of ammonia. I give the sign a respectful nod on my way into town, off for a wine tasting at the Bistrot Parisienne. I have brought a bottle of Cuckmere Valley from Sussex, which is uncorked and decanted around the bar, the atmosphere decidedly frosty. One character unknown to me, mouth set firmly along the contours of his walrus moustache, questions whether English wine is actually made from grapes. Normally I have great faith in Cuckmere Valley, it is dry, crisp, fruity and whoever comes across it by chance soon becomes an habitual drinker. Tonight though, the confidence is slipping away, and I fear it being contemptuously dismissed into a spitoon. With time, the atmosphere mellows, the glasses are topped up and even old walrus face concedes it is not a bad drop. Then like a thunderclap, Philippe le patron affirms the Cuckmere better than many a sauvignon from the south west of France. Soon they are keen to taste the superior Sussex wine which luxuriates in the name Breaky Bottom. Well done you English vintners. In the face of adversity, no subsidies, heavy duty and shite weather you have managed to convert a bar of ever so slightly chauvin Frenchman. Soon to be seen around Rouen the sign 'Ici le vin anglais'.

***

Café society. One cup of coffee entitles you to indefinite residence at a little window on life. The lycée bell rings and there's an influx of students at the Café Metropole, voluminous scarves, cigarettes and excitable laughter. An elegant lady crosses the floor cradling her perfumed bit of fluff, fresh from their appointment at the coiffeur du chien. Mid-morning in the 'Bovary', a dear old goose gives forth on the weather front with all the urgency of an outrider bringing news of the war. Every variation in temperature is chronicled, snow melting then freezing, the Cathedral spire lost to view. Lamenting the demise of the good old fashioned snowboot, she suddenly points her Captain Pugwash profile at the door and is gone. At the 'Bistrot Parisienne' there is Jean-Claude, possessor of one grey jumper and a greatcoat, an amiable monkey capable of launching into unique dance or excruciating song. Round the corner, the terrace at the 'Civet Saint Marc' offers access to all the comings and goings at market, the waiter nonchalantly manoeuvering an enormous tray, steaming cup piled upon steaming cup, finally depositing a big milky coffee in which to dunk my shiny, fresh brioche. Favourite cafés, our own little corners of familiarity and contentment. Sanctuaries from solitude and family life.

**

There is a walk through Rouen which is like a cross section of the urban landscape. The Rue Eau de Robec is an old Norman street with a stream of little bridges and hanging flowers.The water is lost for a while, but carry on East past the Eglise St. Vivien, distinctive for its anarchist symbol on the back of a pew and a stone engraved with every resident priest since the year 1113. Along Rue St. Hilaire there are some beautiful examples of sculpted masonry, and flights of stone stairs leading up the hillside. Towards Darnetal the buildings become more non-descript with second hand car showrooms, boarded up shops and a pigeon loft of a church. Turn right and you are back with the waterway, beneath railway bridges and dual carriageway and beside an enormous grey slab of a bus depot. Here the Robec could dwindle into decay, but a lot of regeneration has gone on with working water mills, freshly laid parkland and a spanking new sports centre. At one point you pass the spot where Gambetta landed his balloon after travelling behind enemy lines in 1870. France was losing the war with Prussia, but he lifted the crowds with a stirring appeal, 'Let us show that if we have not concluded a pact with victory, we have concluded one with death.' A little further along is the 'Moulin de Panneton'. From Medieval times people brought their wheat to be ground in this mill and then baked in the communal oven. A symbol of what was to develop in Rouen with the huge grain silos either side of the Seine. One of these caught fire the last time I visited 'Le Pulqué', the police cut off the road, and we were trapped for hours discussing different ways of cooking duck. With cherries, orange, lemon and lime, lemon and honey, turnips. Duck with turnips? Yes, said Gerard, the juices of the bird take away that sharpness leaving them meltingly tender, and he made that mime of hand to mouth conveying absolute perfection.

The Robec finally disappears beneath a huge viaduct that carries the train to Amiens. To one side the tree-lined slopes of Mont Gargnan, then a great bell tower and on top of the next hill the high rise housing of La Grand'Mare. I returned to L'église St. Julien that evening for their Christmas concert, only to find the doors firmly closed. The previous year I had the same experience at the Cathedral and had to make do with a miserable visit to St.Maclou, where there was no semblance of hearty carols, just the interminable meanderings of a tortured organist. Clearly they are intent on disappointing the non-believer. Tomorrow must return to Brighton to prepare for the Millennial celebrations on the seafront. Such has been the wild weather there is no chance of a sailing; even now oil is pouring onto the

Brittany coastline from a tanker broken in the storm. Instead I experienced the Eurostar train, supersonic speed on the French side and goods wagon trundling back in Blighty. Exasperating but strangely reassuring.

A succession of terrible storms, and with the moon closer and bigger than ever before, the weathermen predicted serious flooding on the South Coast. On Christmas Eve I went down to the beach to check the sandbags outside the café, eight little sacks of hope ranged against the surging sea. Got everything off the floor and locked the café doors against the sky unburdening itself in torrential fashion. No thought of Santa that night, and with daylight, donned wellies and cycled down to the front full of trepidation. Unclicked the padlock, swung open the doors and miraculously the café was dry, the tell-tale line of flotsam stopping just a few yards short of my little domain. At midday we had mince pies and mulled wine, coasting on a high of elation. Over the next few days, word crossed the Channel of a still more ferocious storm over France, with whole forests flattened and the Cathedral at Rouen damaged. The Millennial night approached and the elements calmed to a soft, mild mistiness. A huge firework display, mysterious through the haze, drew thousands of people to the beach, and on the shore a phosphorescent flare burned on and on, lending a magical silouette to the dancing crowd.

Chapter 3

The Fruit of the Earth

Somewhere in the monochrome memories of childhood, a newscast proclaiming the brave new world of the hovercraft, something that could danse across the seas on a cushion of air. Today, the original prototype was brought out of retirement. The interior all brown and stuffy like the Fifties, outside a forlorn figure manually sparking the propellors into life. The magic matress inflated, the engines roared and we scaled the peaks of the sea like a fairground rollercoaster. Forget those brochures of cruise liners sailing serenely to France, roulette wheels spinning and filet mignon served flaming to the table. In deepest January these sparkling acquisitions are resting on the physios couch and the third reserve team come out to play.

Rouen seems to have been spared the worst of the typhoon. The great trees are all standing in the garden of the Musée des Beaux Arts, the swans serenely floating on their pond, and although one of the small spires crashed through the Cathedral roof, the principal spire still soars majestically upto the sky. The Maison de Mule is all safe and secure, and looking out, none of the neighbouring houses appear damaged. There is one house below which lives under a state of seige. The front gate is locked, the front room barred with an iron grill, the upstairs window is permanently hidden behind a metal shutter and the kitchen is confined to an arrow slit of light. At six o'clock the man rolls down the shutter outside the front door and that's them battened down for the night. Paranoia cannot yet be absolute as the roof contains a skylight, completely unprotected. Above it, a view that is totally liberating, the whole of Rouen spread out in a great arc. Late afternoon, the soothing sensation of night gradually encroaching, taking a taper to the city lights. The towers of the Cathedral are illuminated, and soon all around, lamposts and car headlights sparkle and quiver gently. Just occasionally a mist or snowcloud may obscure the view, but otherwise nothing can touch it. A whole vibrant city below, yet apart from the hum of traffic, peel of bells or occasional toot of a train, you are totally dicsonnected, becalmed by the power of the view.

***

Today travelled to Honfleur, a little town on the Channel coast across from Le Havre. West to Lisieux, with its domed Basilica on the hill, then North to Trouville-Deauville on the coast. The train swept across verdant, undulating countryside, the force of the typhoon evident, but nowhere the wholesale devastation seen elsewhere in Normandy. Trouville is quite a pleasant town, with a hill offering expansive views of the white, sandy beaches. The main street is full of restaurants and teashops, and I sat alone on the terrace of the Hôtel du Centre, protected from the teeming rain by a canopy and three enormous outdoor burners. A triumph of hope over adversity. Opposite is the fish market and set aside, a tiny cottage of a perfume shop carrying the scents of Provence. Two pedallo charabancs went by filled with orthodox Jews, all black coats and long sideburns. Perhaps this is the Bournemouth of the French coast.

The bus to Honfleur follows a lovely winding road across the clifftops, past apple orchards, thatched rooves and farms where even the animal houses are built in traditional Norman style. Honfleur centres around a little sheltered harbour, the Capitainnerie du Port a remarkable building risen upon old stone ruins, the entrance adorned with slim turrets and a winding, wooden staircase. This sets the style for much of the town, any one building an amalgam of stone, brick and timber. Wherever you go there is art. Sit on the terrace of the Café Albatross and the table top is an oil impression of the harbour. There is even an old lighthouse given over to art students. Every little lane seems to contain galleries, workshops and potteries although most are aimed at the Parisien rich. The economy hotel was closed and it took a lot of searching to find bed and breakfast for as little as 300 francs. Ultimately a good choice, as the hotel ran an excellent deal with a restaurant called 'La fleur de sel'. Succulent duck terrine, spikily seasoned, with onion marmalade and a salad coated in honey vinigraitte. Rabbit scented with rosemary, served with tart, crisp apple fritters. A light strudel of warm goats cheese wrapped up proceedings for just ninety francs. I strolled out into a friendly bar, then up the cutting to the sea lock where great cargo ships surged past in the dark. Beyond, the twin towers of the Pont de Normandie sent out a pulsating signal into the night.

A tent card at the breakfast table revealed extra charges for everything beyond the standard croissant; a mean-spirited little move. I would love to witness a bill reckoning between la Patronne and one of those Norman peasants legendary for their avarice.

No, you can delete the prunes. I never eat them, they pass straight through me.

But madame, there were three stones beneath your coffee cup.

Gallstones madame. I had a terrible night.

I walked back upto the lock, past a lovely park, and across the sandy beach which looks a bit too exposed for summer sunbathing. From there, you can head uphill behind a diminutive lighthouse, back towards Honfleur. At one point the 'Côte de Grace' divides, cars going one way, pedestrians taking a steep path to the very crest of the town. The view is immense, from open sea to the Pont de Normandie bestriding the Seine estuary. Such is the changing nature of the Norman sky that the docks at Le Havre may be draped in cloud while the bridge sparkles in sunshine. You walk along, past the house where Louis Philippe I spent his last nights before exile in 1848. Then a little sports stadium, and opposite, the Chapel Notre Dame de Grace, with a pilgrims' office and an open air tower of bells mechanically primed to strike the hour, each bell forged with a distinctive motif. Back down the hill, every turning seems to hold a new surprise. One church like a great Norman barn, with seafaring beams supporting curved, wooden arches the length of the building. A majestic modern library, reminiscent of Evreux, a sweeping curve of steel and glass with tall palms reaching for the rafters. Near the harbour, a plaque to Frederic Sauvage who in 1832 invented the propellor at Honfleur. Then another church, quite bedraggled. I enter through a pair of padded doors that finally snap shut, shocking the silence. Not a soul about, but the strange scene of a struggle, smashed fruit, yoghurt pots and baguettes thrown down among the pews, as if some stern prelate had disturbed an illicit picnic.

All the museums were closed for the winter, but there was one exhibition celebrating a century of life in Honfleur. Pre-war football teams squatting in seried ranks, the history of the local cinema and a sign from the old schoolhouse subjecting every innocent activity to the tyranny of hygiene. Do not lick your finger before turning the page. Do not stick your pen up your ear... the list was endless. I will be back when the town is open again, to discover what lies inside the Eric Satie house and the big bubble on the beach that is a Naturedome.

***

The Hag downstairs is back on form. She tried to claim ten thousand francs compensation from the household for the distress caused by an errant cat, a stain on the stair carpet and of course, the cabal of prostitutes working the building. The Palais de Justice threw out the case, and demanded she pay substantial costs in words that brooked no argument. Undeterred, she is compiling a photographic dossier on the activities of the Mule, including constant surveillance of my bike 'illegally' parked in the cellar. Recently, an elderly man moved into the attic flat above, and I feared being sandwiched between two crazies as he was constantly hammering and drilling away. Last night, I was invited up for a cognac, and he has transformed the roof into a palace with majestic furnishings and his own excellent canvases on the walls. Getting up to refill my glass, he delivered an almighty crack to the skull on the old roof beam. He gamely made little of it but the bike felt the thud in the cellar.

This morning off to Fécamp. I once cycled there from Dieppe, taking the quiet D road that scales the hilltops, occasionally dropping down to the resorts dotted along the coast. Today though, it's the early train from Rouen, which involves a change at Breauté-Beuzeville, one of those deserted stations where there is nothing but two tracks and a telegraph operator, black sleeves frantically tapping out a final message to the sheriff. Dawn broke crisp beneath a pinky blue sky as the connecting train pulled away. Fécamp town centre is a bit of a traffic circuit, but there are some pleasant streets around the art museum which is set in a beautiful park. French towns are not big on green spaces, but where they exist they are immaculate sources of tranquility. The museum itself contains little of any value, but no one has told the curator this. The front door is locked and you are followed by a small, stooping woman who traces your every footstep without ever actually looking at you. A few streets further down is the Benedictine Palace, home of the famous liqueur. It shares the delightful flourish and folly of the Royal Pavillion in Brighton, all minarets and grand extravagance. A little way to the right and you are at the harbour, a wide cutting between two steep hillsides, full of yachts, trawlers and old-time sailing ships. The local history of the sea is wonderfully re-enacted at 'La Musée des Terre Neuvas et de la Pêche'. The skills of making barrels and nets. The litany of shipwrecks and rescue on the rocky coast. The words of an orphaned cabin boy providing a graphic account of a long icy voyage to Newfoundland.

About fifteen miles West of Fécamp is Etretat, not much more than a village wedged between clifftops. The bus timetable looked pretty unpromising, so I climbed the hill and tried my luck at hitch hiking. The old thumb has put in sterling service over the years, but my last experience in the Landes region seemed to herald the need for more middle aged modes of transport. I had just finished a 'stage' in the kitchens of Michel Guérard and hitched a lift to Biarritz with a bunch of happy Danes. Black round shades, feet out the window, a production line of big fat reefers, the car careered along towards final, unforgiving impact. Mans' immortality writ large.

Somehow, seven revived religions later, I was still intact as the outskirts of Biarritz sped by. Elation stillborn. The Danish money bag had been left in a café way, way back, and despite gargled protests from the back seat, the car turned around and hurtled back to hell.

The short journey to Etretat held no such terrors, and a good Norman shopkeeper took me there in wonderfully sedate fashion. The cliffs are indeed spectacular. Laminated layers of chalk shining in the sun, harp-shaped pathways worn by the waves, sabre-toothed fragments marooned at sea. Signs on the beach emblazon the perils of incoming tides and falling rocks. 'Danger Vertigo' would be a useful addition because, believe me, if you have never before suffered from heights, the sheer drop at Etretat provides certain initiation. A sort of disorientation sets in as you totter around the clifftops, suddenly realising there is just one tufted footstep between you and oblivion. You indulge in a little mental coaxing to dispel the lure of the abyss and encroaching immobility. All this on a perfectly calm day. Throw in a gale and some dampness underfoot and the experience would be complete.

Back in the village mild euphoria gave way to a sense of exhaustion. Ambled into an olde worlde hotel and drank excellent coffee in front of a hearthful of warm embers. All motivation to move was fast disappearing, but I wanted to reach the station before nightfall and found myself on the platform at Breauté-Beuzeville, watching the sun set red among soft, pillows of cloud. Darkness enclosed the slow, stopping train and at Rouen shards of fog insinuated their way inside the station concourse. I climbed the hill home, half expecting a horse and carriage to come swirling round the corner with Holmes disguised as a coachman. A subtle scent of woodsmoke suffused the flat and I drew the velvet curtains to keep the mist at bay.

***

The next morning the fog lifted, but not before petrifying every last particle of air. A few wisps of mist flirted with the Cathedral spire and the cranes on the docks, rising into a grey dome enclosing every exhalation from the great chimneys of Rouen. These conditions persisted for several days, the dampness penetrating multiple layers of clothing and ultimately the mind. Jean-Claude looked shocked and disoriented by the cold. The patron of the Metropole, normally so upright, who has run the café for nearly sixty years, was unshaven and unable to set up his tables and chairs. Every primal instinct pointed to gathering a few choice nuts and hibernating in a warm quiet place. One step up the evolutionary ladder, I burrowed into the library to discover more about La Cuisine Normande.

It all began in the Year 912 when Charles the Simple, King of Paris, ceded the lands occupied by Rollon the Viking stretching from Cotentin to the Seine. The word Norman derives from Rollon the 'North man'. There has never been a Norman language, but the region acquired a distinctive form of cookery based on three abundant sources; milk, fish and apples. The countryside is so rich in pasture it is said that 'White gold runs through the veins of Normandy'. Strangely, it is nearly impossible to buy fresh milk in the shops, it all goes to making cream, butter and cheese. There are twenty one Norman cheeses, most varieties protected by 'appelation d'origine controlée', a system of quality control similar to wine, defining the region and method of production. A Camembert de Normandie, for example, has to be made from raw milk and a culture of penicillin candidum. Camembert, Pont l'Evêque, Neufchatel and Livarot are considered the four great regional cheeses. Pont l'Evêque and Livarot share a light, clean flavour and a firm but yielding texture. Neufchatel is richer and creamier and comes in various shapes and sizes. The heart-shaped Neufchatel dates back to the Hundred Years War, when French peasant women needed a symbol to express their love for the English soldiers.

Normandy cream and butter possess a wonderful flavour, which helps make Rouen a town famous for patisserie. There are an indecent number of pastry shops around the old market square, their window displays pure works of art. Brioche, a light but rich bread made with butter and eggs, takes pride of place on a Sunday, and there are special pastries for different times of the year. Just now it is the Gâteau du roi, a golden galette of puff pastry baked in the shape of a crown. It dates back to a feast day celebrating the mythical king Saturn. All the ships in port were lit up, every tradesman sent presents to their customers, the bakers bringing cakes to every door. There was music, partying, story telling and all the bells of Rouen rang out. A bean was hidden in the gâteau and whoever found it became king or queen for the day, toasted with the cry of 'Le roi boit'. After the Revolution the festival was briefly renamed 'Galette de la liberté pour les sans culottes'.

A century earlier, that boat from Fécamp with the orphaned boy on board, would probably have been fishing for cod, then preserving the catch at sea. You still see salt cod lying stiff and white at market. Oysters are a relative newcomer to Normandy, but the coastal waters have long been famous for scallops, which hop along the sea bed about seventy yards down. Their fishing is strictly regulated now and a clever scallop can live for up to twenty years. Cream, orange and plump in their shells, they are proudly displayed on the quayside at Dieppe. Mussels are everywhere in the coastal restaurants, enormous tureens keeping you prising and slurping for hours. Just remember to take a flannel and towel. There is a huge variety of fish available, whiting, guernard, bream, red mullet and every type of flat fish. The celebrated 'sole normande' comes with a seafood sauce often cooked in cider. The sauces tend to go overboard on cream and butter, which can smother the delicate flavour of a fish, not to mention the old arteries.

In Normandy, as elsewhere in France, it is almost impossible to eat out if you are vegetarian. Probably the most un-vegetarian dish in the world is 'Tripe à la mode de Caen'. The stomach of an ox, pig or sheep is washed, blanched and cut up small. This is mixed in a big pot with boned calves feet, bacon rind, onion, carrot, garlic and cloves, covered with cider and Calvados, and left to bubble gently all day in a low oven. The liquor is strained over the tripe which is eaten hot or set in its own jelly. Another local speciality is the boudin blanc, a plump white sausage traditionally made from pork, eggs and milk. There are in fact limitless variations, and I have even seen a recipe using fish fillets, roast poultry and calf sweetbreads. The charcutier at the bottom of Rue Beauvoisine boasts an impressive silver trophy beside his tray of boudin blanc. Small consolation on the vegetarian front, the same shop also make an awesome potage de légumes.

With all these savoury dishes you already see the emergence of the apple. Cod sautéed on apple. Duck with baked cinnamon apple. Pork stuffed inside an apple. There is even a day off work to celebrate the mighty apple. The region has twenty principal varieties of eating apple with lyrical names like Muscadet de Dieppe and La Doux Joseph. Cookers are a seperate breed-Clochard, Rambaud, Bénédictin-used to make the famous Tarte Normande. Every dessert menu carries this dish and none taste alike. Some are meltingly soft, others charred to a caramelised crispness. For cider making, finely tuned palates catagorise the apples for their sweet, sour, bitter and acid qualities. Most ciders are drawn from 40% bitter and 40% sweet apples, the balance providing the distinctive flavour. A great deal of local cider is distilled and aged in wood to produce Calvados. 'Le trou Normand' is the tradition of drinking a tot of old 'calva' between the courses of a large meal, the liqueur stimulating the stomach to make way for the next dish. Everywhere you see the 'le trou normand' above a dinky restaurant, cottage or boutique, but really it is just the local ploy to facilitate a big feed.

Across the region there are posters celebrating Maupassants' 150th birthday. He understood the integral role of food in Norman heritage, linking the land with the rhythm of daily life and even shaping how the world is perceived.

'I love this country and I love to live here, because this is where my roots lie, deep, delicate roots which attach a man to the land where his ancestors lived and died, attach him to a way of thinking and eating, the customs and foods, the local peasant dialect, the distinctive smell of the earth, the villages and the air itself.'

'Le Horla'

***

Arrived at Neufchatel en Bray in the teeth of the storm. The lights of the bus pulled away to leave the Mule a solitary figure in the sweeping rain, the town apparently closed against the night, nestling within the comfort of its tall pitched rooves. Only the hotel opposite the church appeared open, and although the frontage looked a bit dowdy, the offer of bed, breakfast and evening meal for just 240 francs was more than welcome. Daylight revealed a little town among rolling hills with the cobbled main street a backwater in time. Petrol served by an attendant in a white coat and a grubby monument celebrating one hundred years of colonial rule in Algeria. Great banks of cloud were once again breaking over the horizon and I hurried into the church to escape the deluge. The stained glass windows were magnificent in the semi-darkness, and by candlelight you could make out a plaque reminiscent of August 1914, when with the Germans just 15 kilometres away, prayers were sent upto our Lady of Lourdes to preserve the town from invasion. Hailstones gave way to clear sky and I walked out down the hill to the River Béthune, not much more than a stream running through a sprawl of industrial workshops. Beyond the town, its banks give way to rich pastureland, source of all that is special on the Norman table.

Pommeréval is just a scattering of houses around a crossroads, one wall bearing the inscription, 'White Charolais calf stolen two weeks ago. According to intelligence it should return'. A little way along beside the sixteenth century church, is a dairy farm where Madame Dujardin has lived all her life. The milk from her fifty cattle passes through the milking shed to 'le laboratoire' where it is whisked into cream. For butter, the cream is held for five days, churned in a broad barrel, shaped with wooden moulds and wrapped in paper bearing the farms' own emblem. Fromage blanc is also made here, in huge great tubs, and there is quite a novelty product, 'confiture du lait', where milk is cooked slowly with sugar to achieve the deep colour of caramel. After an appreciative tasting, madame led me across the milking yard to a little stall that was home to a day-old calf. It nuzzled up all warm and playful.

Next stop, a local cheese farm. There is a cluster of them around Nesle Hodeng, not far south of Neufchatel, and I opted for La ferme des Fontaines. I latched onto a tour for a busload of English schoolkids, who were clearly oblivious to all that was being said. Part of the glazed look was down to Madame, a martyred soul with doleful delivery. We have no weekends, no holidays, no life, but endure it all to maintain the traditional ways. The talk over, she shut the door on my beak and I went off to the nearby Monnier farm to buy a heart-shaped Neufchatel. Visit the basement of the museum at Neufchatel and you discover how the cheese has been made for centuries. The curd thickened then drained over a cradle, squeezed in a wooden press, shaped in copper moulds, then dusted with salt and left to mature in the cellar.

Not far away at St. Saire, is Au Clos du Bourg, an apple orchard in the process of organic conversion. Etienne Lurois used to work for an industrial cereal farm, became disillusioned and planted his orchard ten years ago with twenty different varieties of apple. He has found it no more expensive to cultivate organically. Left to her own devices, Nature produces a balance of insects that leaves the fruit unscathed; it is only when you introduce pesticides that certain insects become dominant and damage the crop. Most flavour lies beneath the skin, so for cider making it is important to let the skin and pulp mascerate for several hours before pressing. All the necessary yeast and sweetness is provided by the apple, and the juice is left to ferment in huge vats before bottling. At the end of the barn are rows of oak barrels maturing Calvados and Pommeau, a younger, milder version of Calva that has been blended with apple juice. Etienne built the barn himself using colossal, old wooden beams. He has a refreshingly unmaterialistic approach to life, content to fashion the things he loves but virtually disinterested in marketing them.

About ten miles further south, near Sommery, is a pig farm with its own charcuterie. The pigs at La Ferme de Peau de Leu are reared on straw without growth promoters, and fed on cereals. I bought some roast pork and smoked sausage and asked if I could take a look inside the pig houses. Ordinarily it would mean a compulsory shower and change of clothes, but if I just peeked through a gap in the barn, I could watch the pigs in my unkempt state. There they were, big happy porkers, snorting, chomping and rolling around, all of a sudden standing back, trotters aloft, to indulge in a spot of line dancing. I carried on to the lovely little town of Buchy, sat outside a café and ate my farmhouse cheese and sausage with a refreshing glass of kir pêche.

***

Rouen town hall is a grand place, fronted by acres of shiny flagstones and an impressive statue of Napoleon on horseback. Best viewed through autumn leaves from the terrace of the Café Hôtel de Ville. Behind it is a secluded park with giant trees gently sloping above hillocks and pathways. You can get there by a circuitous little route, uphill towards the fountain cascading through heroic figures of man and beast, right before the dome of the Lycée Corneille, past ancient houses and a monastery, and finally down through the park gates into a setting of total tranquility. At night the Hôtel de Ville is lit up amid sparkling torrents of water and skateboarders surfing the pavement, always dismounted attempting the spectacular at Bonapartes' plinth, hanging hoods loping after their wheelies running wild and free.

Across the square is O'Kallaghans bar. The Frenchman who owns it has done his homework; Guiness is patiently poured to leave a deep head indented with the shamrock, tasting as good as anything outside of Ireland, and the evening always ends with a rasping rendition from The Pogues. The place is popular with a young French crowd and also the sizeable British contingent who work and study in Rouen. The English abroad can be an ignorant embarassment, but here they are a pleasure to know, multi-lingual, open-minded and keen to travel beyond the normal confines of beach and sun. The pub is all geared up with a giant sports screen, which reflects a new wave in France. Prior to the semi final of the '98 World Cup, football was far from the national sport, but now every top match is followed in partisan fashion. Go into any bar and there may be two TV's perched aloft, any newcomer locking into the screen as if instructed by some higher force. All just about credible with a big game, but every tedious sport commands the same rapt attention, the world absorbed in darts, curling and snooker, oblivious to the smashing glass as a rogue skateboard comes hurtling through the window.

***

There is plenty to see on the waterways South of Rouen. First stop Pont de l'Arche, where the Seine meets the River Eure. If you ever need to use Rouen coach station, time your arrival just before departure, because it is a bleak, dispiriting place, a bunker filled with engine fumes and the constant bleeping of buses as they manoeuvre in and out of their narrow bays. Pacing up and down, you strive to construct an image that will take you out of this place, but the grey torpor takes hold, your mind seals over, the clock face frozen in time. Eventually, that final minute clicks on, the bus revs up, and you are away beneath the hill at Bonsecours, meandering through the plains and hamlets that border the Seine. Pont de l'Arche is a little town with a clutch of cobbled streets and a butchers' window advertising 'beef and horse'. There is a tower, an armoury and a church with a grand organ, modern wooden sculptures and lines of pews with their own little gates.

A few miles downstream, one bank rises up with chalk cliffs and tree-lined hills, the other becomes a delta of lakes, tributaries and pretty villages. Tornedos has a tiny town hall that must have been built by children. There are solid cottages with a few ducks and hens pottering around an old water pump. At Poses, the pleasure steamer 'William the Conqueror' is all brightly painted ready for the new season. This is a lively little place with boating, water skiing and one of those blue collar restaurants that are great value for money. Unlimited bread and wine, hors d'oeuvres platter, main course, salad, fruit and cheese, all for fifty five francs. It would be pointless asking for a menu as the main course is always a slab of meat. Requesting a non-meat meal would only set the chef to staring blankly as he caressed the blade of his boning knife. I remember when an apprentice in Nice, the entire complement of staff, Madame Argentier, Bernard the waiter and me, sitting down to eat before each meal service. Invariably it would be steak sitting in a pool of blood. I would carefully select those surfaces that had at least seen fleeting contact with the grill, but even these defied mastication, eventually re-appearing as shame-faced gristle on the side of the plate. Well, this piece of meat at Poses was remarkably tender, slipping down a treat with chunky homemade chips and copious amounts of red wine. The onward journey around 'Le Lac des deux Amants' was a little sluggish, but what a delightful name to be intoxicated over. Then on through Léry, a few pleasant streets and a twelfth century church with a hebrew inscription above the alter. A few miles further along is Val de Reuil, 'ville contemporain', a dormitory town that has been dropped in the middle of nowhere. There are plenty of trees and sports pitches within the estates, but none of the buildings meld together, the concrete is already discoloured, and however you look, there is no beauty here. You sense the future as a corroding bantustan.

The next day I took the train one stop further down the line to Gaillon. The road rises through woodland, the air filled with chain saws trying to make sense of the carnage wrought by the storm. Beyond Villers-sur-le-Roule you emerge high above the river, with trees and clouds reflected in the still water. A lone duck ploughs along mid-stream, its wake parting in perfect symmetry. Approaching Tosny is like discovering a Medieval fortress, with thick stone houses behind tall, stone walls. There is a silent schoolhouse and a farmhouse brewery you imagine had been there for centuries. In fact, Monsieur Duplessi only started brewing his 'Richard Coeur de Lion' last year, the vats all sparkling and clinically clean. The scrupulous hygiene, essential when making a beer without addidtives, does nothing to diminish the earthy quality of his bronze coloured malt.

Down the hill there is a racecourse and then a willowy hollow with a miniature railway and donkeys munching the grass. A few miles on a suspension bridge slopes smoothly across the river offering a dramatic approach to the cliffs at Les Andelys, a massive, sheer chalkface topped with the ruins of a castle. The restaurant beneath the cliff was full of lorry drivers, fresh from their latest exploits blockading the French highways, this time over the 35 hour week. On face value France seems a model of civility, order even deference, but during my two winters here, there has hardly been a section of society that has not taken to the streets. Farmworkers, nurses, firemen, lycée students, their struggle shaped in the historic language of solidarity and martyrdom. In todays' paper, the 1200 fishermen of the Seine estuary pledged to fight a new port development that would threaten their fish stocks. 'In all events, we might die, but not alone. We will fight on till the end.' Appropriate inspiration as I began a slow and measured ascent of the perpendicular path up the cliff. From the castle walls there is a view to savour. Waterways coursing through wooded islands, under the flowing bridge, and then the pretty houses of Les Andelys nestling within a curve of the river, that meanders on beneath imperious white headlands. You could imagine every Norman baron itching to include this corner in their fiefdom, commanding the river trade and all the land beyond. Above the castle, the panorama grows still more expansive. On and up, through a small forest, tangibly thinning air, and then implausibly, the stadium of Les Andelys football club. The French may be short on humour, but they remain masters of the absurd.

Back at base, Le Petit Andelys is a delightful waterfront of old Norman houses, leading to an imposing stately home, with a huge domed entrance and two majestic linden trees. At the very least the summer residence of Le President de la République. Mais non, the local retirement home, and next to it a bright, new hospital with rich green lawns rolling down to the Seine. Equally impressive is the old, wood-panneled splendour of the Hôtel de la Chaîne d'Or, which owes its name to the old ferry that linked the river banks before the days of the bridge. Such was the value of the crossing, it was said to provide a pot of gold for the local coffers. Today, the riches lie within the hotel dining room, where cigars, brandy glasses and dinner jackets luxuriate long into the afternoon. A chill twilight gradually enveloped the quayside, and it was with some anxiety that I awaited the last bus back to Gaillon. Was I standing at the right spot, or working from an obsolete timetable? But here it comes, pneumatic doors swinging open, off to the gare de Gaillon with an hour to spare. I sat quietly in the station café with a docile giant of a dog for company. The train drew in and I snuggled up, eyes closed, head gently tingling with the light, caressing tones of the girl opposite.

***

The beginning of February and a Spring-like morning on the terrace of Café Metropole. Digesting a choice morsel of information that the patron has just divulged. Before the war, Jean-Paul Sartre and Simone de Beauvoir used to inhabit a corner of the café, he a lecturer at Le Havre, she teaching at the local lycée. At the time Monsieur Olivier was too preoccupied with young girls to pay much attention to a couple of eggheads, and has since had relations with customers that were 'beaucoup plus solides'. But imagine, at perhaps the very table where I munch my morning croissant, sat two of the great minds of the twentieth century. I just happen to have finished Sartres' childhood autobiography, 'Les Mots', where by his own admission he was a spoilt, friendless, ugly child, never known to kick a football around, much less score a winning goal. An inauspicious start that gives us all hope.

Rouen does possess a strong literary tradition. Flaubert and Maupassant were both local boys made good, but probably the greatest claim to fame lies with the seventeenth century writer Pierre Corneille. You can still visit his house, beautifully preserved on the Rue de la Pie, just West of the old market square. Pull the bell and you are welcomed in by a self-effacing woman, who conducts a personalised tour up three flights of a winding staircase. On each floor the doors are unlocked to reveal his portraits, a library with every first edition, and in one room, an intricate model of the bustling market square. Corneille did most of his writing at Petit Quévilly on the Rive Gauche, met the young Moliére directing a theatre troupe in Rouen, and finally left to spend his declining years in Paris. Did she ever tire of telling her tale, up and down the same staircase? 'No, it is like any job. There is repetition.' We bade farewell, the front door closed, and I tried to imagine her wrapped inside the quiet house, boundless time occasionally broken by the bell.

Corneille and the classical repetoire feature strongly at Le Théâtre des Deux Rives, but you can find every type of performance art in Rouen. Opera, wacky danse, film festivals from countries you might never associate with film. All integrated across the region, so that in the depths of the Pays de Bray there might be a village hall, with a magic lantern projecting the cinema of South Africa or Vietnam.

***

Pockets of air caught between the seasons. A friendly breeze wafting through the blossom liberates those layers of clothing that have constrained us for so long. The ancient statues in the Musée d'Antiquités brighten in the sunlight amid a carpet of mauve flowers. A human relic perched on a stone dozes amid the soft sensation of warmth. A man with a dog distances himself from a young amorous couple who offer him a piece of their pizza. A few hours later the mean wind is back, primed with damp and cold, but the shackles of winter have been loosened and soon we will walk carefree, heads tilted upwards, balcony windows thrown open, bare feet reveling in their new found freedom. The burgeoning spring brings a feeling of envy as most of my discoveries have been caught between wind and rain, and now limitless numbers of people will be able to explore Normandy the easy way, showered by apple blossom, smelling the warmth emanating from the deep, green pasture.

On my last day before returning to Brighton seafront, a group of us went down to Le Pulqué, to discover the place closed. Custom had dwindled to a nothingness, and Gerard Gomez with all his tales and years of experience is off to work in a canteen. First the Café de la Grande Poste now the dear old Pulqué. Jean-Paul knew of a nearby restaurant inside a wholesale food market. The main room was alive

108

with market traders and restaurateurs, but we settled into a more select corner where for an extravagant 90 francs a head there was a trio of terrines, cod and salmon in a sorrel sauce, the ripest of local cheeses and a strawberry tart. I had intended to go to a talk that afternoon by the moustachioed sheep farmer José Bové celebrated for burning down a McDonalds and upbraiding the world economic order at Seattle, but all that food, a succession of pitchers of wine and the effort of keeping up with a conversation involving a bright comedienne and two slick-tongued Frenchmen, depleted the old brain cells and a siesta was compulsory.

Got to Le Havre a couple of hours before the night boat pulled out, and dined a solitary figure in a restaurant with the most excruciating decor-lurid green carpet, pink tableclothes, wires tumbling through slats in the ceiling and two alligators stuck on the wall. The owner shuffling round in Stan Ogdens' slippers. Remarkably the food was really good, culminating in a seminal tarte normande. I booked into a 'reclining seat' on the boat, but the pervasive night light, horse hair blanket and unyielding upholstery of a seat that refused to recline, all spelt doom, and I upgraded to a cabin with a porthole. It brought to mind the final pages of Maupassants' 'Pierre et Jean', when a huge crowd lined the quayside at Le Havre to wave off a new liner bound for New York. No fanfare tonight, but there was something primal about watching, naked, as the silent city slipped away, a rotating arc of light guiding the ship out to sea.

Rouen from Bonsecours Hill

Statues and fountains outside Le Musée des Antiquités

Statues outside Le Musée des Antiquités

Garden behind the Hôtel de Ville

Le quartier St. Maclou

L'Ecole des Beaux-Arts

L'Hôtel de Bourgtheroulde

The Cathedral at Rouen

The Cathedral at Rouen

Garden of Le Musée de Céramique

Barbier de Sa Ville

Watchmaker Rue Beauvoisine

Patron of the Café Métropole

Bistro Parisien

L'Eglise Jeanne d'Arc

Quartier des Antiquaires

Le Rideau Rouge

Bonsecours Obelisk

The Romany Fair

Rouen through the mist

Rouen Docks

The Seine, west of La Bouille

Les Andelys

Jumièges

Honfleur

Etretat

Victor Hugo's house at Villequier

Lake at Forges-les-Eaux

Swimming Pool at Forges-les-Eaux

The bird park at Clères

Gerberoy

Rural Life in Le Pays de Bray

Rural Life in Le Pays de Bray

Rural Life in Le Pays de Bray

The goat farm at Bellencombre

The grounds of Château Vascoeuil

The grounds of Château Vascoeuil

Château Martainville

Boat up on the hill, in the grounds of Château Robert le Diable

Europe's oldest oak tree at Alouville

Chapter 4

Summer in Rouen

The third Sunday in May, Dieppe Market comes to town, and for one day Brightonians transform their shopping habits, smelling cheeses, pressing fruit, savouring slices of dried sausage and carrying away thousands of baguettes on sturdy bicycles garlanded with onions. The same day is Mackerel Fayre, when the towns' small fishing fleet collect on the shore for the ancient ritual of the blessing of the nets. Last year, glorious sunshine presided over both events, Alan and Sams' colourful boats bobbing gently just a hundred yards from my kitchen where mackerel were turning bluey black on the charcoal grill. This year the rain is falling in waves and I am not on the seafront. Two days ago the restaurant was sold. A long season beside a hot stove takes its toll and the prospect of life in Rouen has been seditiously enticing. The final menu for a musical night at the Brighton Festival, had a touch of invention about it. Ricotta éclair on a wild mushroom sauce; plaice filled with ginger and banana served on a tomato and coriander sauce. All to the deep, soothing vocals and double bass of the jazz duo 'Something Cool'. I spent the next day totting up the closing stock, and saying goodbye to the arch that harbours the restaurant. Originally hewn out of chalk cliffs one hundred and fifty years ago, the smooth shape and faded brickwork exude a primal feeling of earthiness. Wandered about the walls, mused over time and thought fond thoughts.

Arrived in Rouen amid soft rain, gentle warmth and a feeling of nascent summer. Velvety red roses in the yard outside the house and a boat for sale on the pavement. For the next four nights there will be open air performances of Shakespeare films on a giant, white screen in front of the town hall. Tonight Orson Welles, tomorrow Al Pacino, all part of the Festival Jeanne d'Arc. She is of course everywhere in Rouen, plaques on the dungeon and cathedral walls reveal different points of captivity, and a monument outside the stunning, modern église Jeanne d'Arc marks the site of her final demise. Yet I cannot get excited by her and it seems neither could the French, until such time long after her death, when it became politic to point the finger of blame at the English. It is strange how modern secular movements should identify with a Medieval, religous zealot. In the visitors' book at the Musée Jeanne d'Arc two English lesbians have claimed her as their own. The museum is an uninspiring collection of waxworks, but the Rue Jeanne d'Arc is more worthwhile. Ten years ago, traffic poured down it in a pulsating throb of exhaust pipes, but the local authority has progressively discouraged the car, and the road is currently being dismantled to make way for a greenified pathway through town.

On the right hand side leading down from the station, is a sign pointing to L'église St.Patrice. It is a simple old engraved sign, no logo or corporate sponsor, indicating a 16th century church famous for its stained glass windows. I have often tried to visit the church but each time the wooden door has been firmly bolted. There has always been the compensation of wandering the neighbouring streets with their sloping facades, old school playground alive with sound, and 'Le barbier de sa ville'. Step inside and the place is filled with barberesque memorabilia – shaving brushes, puffer sprays and an amazing collection of art deco advertisements portraying slick coiffure as the source of self-esteem. The phone bell rings and it might have been Humphrey Bogart calling. The barber replies in deadpan fashion; resident for twenty three years he has never felt the need to cultivate small talk. He does however possess an original line in music, which is pleasantly distracting when the old cut throat is flashing about the gizzard region.

Walk back down the Rue Jeanne d'Arc, and on the other side is the Palais de Justice. The ornate gothic exterior is simply magnificent, and there is nothing to stop you venturing inside the palace itself. Up a stone staircase and into a vast hall, with a sweeping wooden roof like an upturned ships' hull. Along passageways with magisterial courtrooms, the office of the vice-President of the Counsel, lawyers in full regalia and a beautiful, handcuffed prisoner being hurried away to an infinitely worse place. To look at the Palais de Justice you imagine it has passed unscathed through the turmoil of time, and stands as it was conceived in the fourteenth century. In fact the building was severely damaged by wartime bombing, and what you see today is the result of outstanding restoration work. Only when the repairs were virtually complete did they discover an even older structure beneath the courtyard; the Jewish Monument. You can visit it on a Saturday afternoon, stepping down in time to find the walls, windows and pillars virtually intact, finally descending a winding staircase to place your feet on an earthen floor that is nine hundred years old. The purpose of the building is a question that has absorbed the tour guide for decades. Was it a school, a library, a synagogue? Competing academic theories are examined at great length, the initial sense of wonderment wearing off as you become aware that a one and a half hour lecture inside a dank, airless dungeon is no way to spend your Saturday afternoon. Ultimately the solution to the archaeological riddle provides no great excitement. The monument was a house, a wealthy house with a kitchen. What they cooked in that kitchen would have been interesting, but I stifled the question, anxious to return above ground. The guide looked rather crestfallen as the little group vapourised into the sunlight, no one stopping to buy his book. We had already heard the book, but there was something admirable, a lost quality, about his meticulous endeavour to understand the past.

***

A ferocious gale swept through the night bringing

with it a deluge of cold rain. Undeterred, the Mule ventured forth to Le Tréport in the northernmost corner of Normandy. One little train sprinted across wooded pastureland to Abancourt, then after an hour in a lonely waiting room, another followed the river Bresle up towards the sea. Clouds raced across the sky, occasionally unleashing a torrent of rain against the window, finally clearing as the train drew in just short of the waves. Le Tréport lies in a wide valley not dissimilar to Fécamp. The fishing port is less pretty, but either side the cliffs are spectacular, massive swathes of chalk rising high above the town.

The church sits halfway up the hill, like an indomitable fortress, and I was about to continue on up when a sudden squall sent me scurrying for shelter. I landed inside a fish restaurant with a special menu for what turned out to be Mothers' Day in France, 'La fête des mamans'. L'assiette du capitaine contained 'amandes', like little oysters, and 'bulots' that are prised out of their curly shells all sweet, earthy and muscular. A procession of families took their place, the first containing three generations of mother, the oldest a worn and faded vision of the future. Each took their order from the economy menu; celebration is one thing, but there is no need to be reckless. One old couple did push the boat out, with a bottle of bubbly nestling in an ice bucket, but barely a word was exchanged between them, the silence broken only when papa admonished the waiter for some criminal misdemeanour over a crustacean.

Next up a mother, two sons and one spouse, the

unmarried son clearly the dysfunctional figure. Bizarrely decked out in shades, prone to inappropriate gestures and incapable of safely pouring the wine, older brother took charge of the ordering. It was here that maman directed her attention. He may have married a girl with the profile of a pelican, but at least he had achieved something in life. The wastrel meanwhile, was helplessly trying to rearrange the bulot pronger he had irredeemably bent out of shape. Last upto the door, a trio struggling against the wind. They eventually managed to seat grandma who was something of an unwitting participant in proceedings. Pink slippers, sackcloth shift, mouth folded upon her chin. Daughter berating her husband for being late, and their son desperate to be anywhere but there. Outside, on the floor, in the toilet, a corruscating 'Restes-là!!' stifled his final bid for freedom. La fête des mamans rolled on.

The stairway up the clifftop was quite a climb, but once there the view was breathtaking. Great lines of surf sweeping upto the coast, clouds casting islands upon the sea. The walk west towards Dieppe was exhilarating, the young, green corn thrashing around in a frenzy, but ultimately the wind drained the old leg muscles, carrying the Mule back towards town. Tucked away beneath the church, the museum is housed within a turret that used to serve as the towns' keep. Over time there have been many associations with Britain. 'Les grelots', the stones uniquely abundant on the local shoreline, were once invaluable in making Cornish porcelain. An anonymous English benefactress funded the towns' first lifeboat, and in the First World War the English set up a huge encampment on the front. Images of the next war reveal terrible devastation and a beach bristling with mines and barbed wire.

Coming out of the museum you pass the Rue d'Enfer. Call me old-fashioned but a tent on the cliff face would be preferable to setting up house on the 'Road from Hell'. Nothing quite that terrible on the seafront, just the normal collection of chips and candyfloss interspersed with seafood restaurants. The beach itself is stoney and uninviting, lined with a hideous stretch of peach-coloured flats that obscures the pretty cluster of streets huddled beneath the cliff. The journey home was memorable. Black cloud flirted with evening sunshine and a double rainbow took hold across the valley. This was no fleeting appearance; all the way back to Abancourt the train trundled through an enchanted setting of farmhouses, water mills, fishing boats and grazing cattle, all captured within that magnificent 'arc du ciel.'

***

Summer on hold. A day of incessant rain that defied the protective power of any umbrella. Spent the morning in the Chambre de Commerce trying to find out how to set up a business in France. It was like something out of a Kafka novel. For every enquiry you were sent down labyrinthine corridors to an office where a tightly controlled madame, generally overdone in the make up and shoulder pad department, overwhelmed you with circulars relating to employment law, the 35 hour week, the right of previous employees to continue on your payroll, the minimum wage at forty francs seventy two centimes an hour, five different types of drinks license, five judicial structures for small businesses... I ran out before even broaching the regulations on environmental health, took the stairs to avoid the automated voice in the lift, landed in a basement cul de sac, broke through the fire door, fled the alarm and lost a shoe in a suction puddle. Plodded home to wait for the France Telecom engineer who never came, and stared out at the huge cruise liner berthed in the middle of town, 'Seaborne Sunshine'. I scrunched newspaper into my shoes, ran a bath and went to bed with bear.

The next day saw a return to temperate normality. Tentative at first, then wholesomely warm, by evening the café terraces were alive, street musicians appeared and it was as if Rouen had only ever known summertime. Encouraged, I decided to leave next morning for a cycle ride through the Pays de Bray. The hedgerows were filled with the scent of elderflower and orange blossom, the fields awash with buttercups. This is a region of lovely rolling countryside occasionally opening out to verdant plains abounding with sheep and cattle. Most villages possess a post office, café and shop, and often a little town hall with l'école des garçons on one side and l'école jeunes filles on the other. I meandered north from Serqueux to Bully then across to Mesniéres-en-

Bray. At the bottom of the village is a château in beautiful grounds with exotic peacocks and black swans. I signed up for the grand tour, but soon realised that after eight hours in the saddle my mind could no longer absorb whether a pillar was renaissance or gothic, or why the confessional in the chapel had only one door. The old body craved comfort and I escaped across the yard, over the moat and off to find lodgings in Neufchatel.

Above the town, tucked away under the hillside, is the Cellier du Val Bourg, a collection of farmhouses and old barns that once stored the local cider. For 250 francs I got a luxurious room overlooking the farmyard, with copper beech and willow trees casting long shadows in the evening sunlight. At breakfast I got into conversation with the owner, Xavier. He recounted how a friend of his, who works for a top-notch restaurant in London, believes the level of haute cuisine in England to be more ambitious and imaginative than in France. Converstaion ceased and cutlery froze across the breakfast room. I imagine the full complement of native guests left without paying, but Xavier went on to talk about the possibility of producing an organic Neufchatel on the farm, and a friend who recently started a farmhouse brewery. I met him the next day at 'La Comice d'agriculture', a big annual outing where all the countryside comes to town, buying, selling and competing for prizes. L'élevage Dujardin was commended for its cream and butter and Etienne Lurois won the Pommeau prize. There were a few stalls of local produce, but principally the event was devoted to livestock in every guise. Parading, feeding, suckling, smelling, generally looking lost and out of place. The brewer was a real enthusiast with samples of six different beers and a pocketful of roasted barley. Next month he is hosting a big party with swordfighting, archery contests and fire eaters. Come dressed as a Viking and you get in for free.

About twenty miles south of Neufchatel, all roads converge in the centre of Forges-les Eaux. Not an auspicious beginning, but it is worth persevering with this little town as there is a lot to discover that is surprisingly peaceful. Behind the town hall is a park lined with beautiful buildings that once accomodated Cardinal Richlieu and Louis XIII when they descended on Forges to take the waters. Today it is a place of deep shade and tranquility, a wonderful setting to knock a ball about the tennis court.

Over the crossroads and down the road to Dieppe, there is a discrete turning left. A lane runs past golden ponies and a grand old house now fallen upon hard times, the upstairs shutters all rotten and askew. Up a gentle slope, L'Hospice Beaufils, a homely cottage hospital with a baby orchard being nurtured into life. A little further along, a disused railway track crosses the main road, disappearing inside a long, cool canopy of trees, bedded in bracken and filled with birdsong. I seem to have bissected this railway several times these past few days, and it may be the most unspoilt way of discovering the Pays de Bray.

Forges is famous for gambling. In the mid nineteenth century the Cappucine convent was turned into a cardschool and later the Casino was built. A collection of magnificent buildings, some new some old, it is fronted by La Porte de Gisors, a beautiful edifice which is all that remains of a Carmelite convent following wartime bombardment. The gateway was bought by the Casino, transported the thirty odd miles from Gisors and reconstructed in immaculate style. Two convent conversions not as originally intended. Across the road is another lone edifice, this time in the grounds of an open air swiming pool. Take a dip, look around and you realise you are back in teenage territory with shouts of bravado and circles of smoke puffed in the air. A little further down is Le Lac des Andelles, the silence of the lake only disturbed by the rustling of trees and the odd duck making a break for the water. On the banks, a bust of the young aviator Oliver Montalent has gone missing and been replaced with a Millennial sculpture of three women stretching for the sky. Across town is the Museum of the Resistance and Liberation, carrying images of the war in Normandy and beyond. A French street draped in swastikas, a radio control box and a basket for carrying birds. Messages of untold consequence carried on the foot of a pigeon.

South east of Forges you enter the Oise region and a crop of historic villages. Songeons 'let us dream' is a dip in the hillside garlanded in flowers. At the top of the street is La Ferme de St. Aubin with a grand old gate portraying bread baked in a wood oven. It lies on the Green Meridien that runs through the heart of France from Dunkerque to the Eastern Pyrenees. Next weekend, every town and village along the Meridien is holding a communal picnic and the farm should have an enviable hamper with its cheese, cider and organic chicken. A few miles away, a lane of sculpted hedgerows leads to the ancient village of Gerberoy, a handful of cobbled streets adorned with rose tree cottages. Behind the manor house, a terraced garden descends like a Tuscan hillside. A cool avenue of trees skirts beneath the village to a farmyard stirring with ducklings and geese. There is some evidence of activity in this remarkable little place, an exhibition of art and a fiesta of Spanish music, but the enduring impression is one of absolute peace.

West and north the road opens out through fields of peas and young sweetcorn, arriving at Haussez a village of deep lanes and thick stone walls. Follow the signs for 'rhubarbe' to a farmyard with a big white horse and an open carriage, the horse in uneasy session with the hoof doctor. Inside the barn, all is animation as about twenty guests tuck into Madame Dufrennes' brioche, jam and rhubarb rosé. She has carved a happy living out of rhubarb, concocting endless varieties of jam as well as specialities like dandelion flower, parsley jelly and onion confit. I have always thought of rhubarb as quintessentially English, but it is obviously quite at home in Normandy and actually originates from Mongolia and Tibet. Outside, the horse is hooved and harnessed, the guests clamber onto the charabanc and roll out of the farmyard united in song. A picture of simple contentment that somehow belies the modern world.

***

A warm, peaceful evening on the little terrace outside the Bistrot Parisien. Look left, and the setting sun makes a striking silouette of the great tree outside the old pharmacy, a lovely, wood-framed building lined with forlorn statues. Look right and the deep foliage of Mont Gargnan shimmers beneath a clear, blue sky. People pass by, pullovers casually draped about shoulders, a meticulous French art, soft leather attaché cases swinging their way home. I watch distractedly as Jean-Claude, the semi-derelict, hares round the corner clutching a shiny, portable computer. A shifting population needs to stay in touch.

Hélas, this beautiful bubble in time must end. There is a crust to be earned. I visited one estate agent specialising in the restaurant trade, but they had nothing remotely attractive to offer. The main man cultivated a slick of hair across his bare head, a moustache making common cause with his sideburns and an absolute quality of oiliness. His associate hovered in the background, emerging now and then to administer a polish to the principal ego. 'Monsieur V has a very fine Jaguar! Ha Ha!' And they fell into a round of extravagantly pronouncing the word Jaguar. Monsieur V cut to pensive pose, eyes moving laterally across his face as a sequence of squalid kitchens passed before him. I decided to look elsewhere.

Early for an appointment at another estate agent, I strolled around the Ile de Croix, the island in the middle of Rouen that somehow gets overlooked. At one end there are moorings for pleasure craft and at the other, a majestic iron railway bridge that beats to the roll of a thousand goods wagons. I arrived at an office furnished with antique desks, faded velvet wall coverings and a vast collection of signed photographs of stars from the Fifties's. It seems the owner grew up in a casino where Edith Piaf once came to play. Ultimately though, all this finery flattered to deceive and I was forced to look again. José a Portugese restaurateur, recommended a third estate agent, and this one had a restaurant for sale on one of Rouen's oldest streets, a little stream down one side and a game of boules on the other.

***

A beautiful day and the bus climbed over the Pont de Normandie, to discover Honfleur a town transformed. The café terraces alive with colour, expansive parasols raised like sails in the harbour. Decided to do the tourist thing and visit the sites that had all been sealed up in January. 'La maison Sartie' is a surreal experience of sound and imagery. You don a high-tec audio cassette which somehow complements whatever is going on around you. A flying pear, a magic roundabout, a monkey dressed as a waiter inviting you to the ball. A white piano tinkles away in a white room, daylight revealed then shut away, simple statements and quirky humour all redolent of John Lennon. I ran into a party of old people who had been infected by the folly of it all, tumbling out into the courtyard laughing and cackling. I bought a flying pear, a CD and a folding parchment of the pictures, all ultimately disappointing. This was an experience to savour for the moment.

After the fun of Satie, the mainstream Boudin museum was worthy but rather dull. People seem to develop a reverence in the presence of great art, smiling faintly, walking backwards, nodding their respect. A whispering gallery, with a beautiful Rodin statue and famous impressions of the harbour. The sun beckoned and I took a boat trip under the bridges linking the waterways of Honfleur. Old oak hulks, some restored to former glory, others broken beyond repair. Blue and white boat houses with verandas, the sea lock and a modern monolith topped with a mushroom that controls all the shipping across the estuary. The view of the town from the water is quite beautiful, the pretty houses nestling beneath the Côte de Grace. All development has been banned on the hillside, a prohibition to be proud of.

I took a little turn around the harbour which everywhere reflects the long seafaring heritage. Cavernous salt cellars, a fourteenth century fishing museum and a memorial to Samuel Champelin who in 1608 left Honfleur and discovered Quebec. This heritage is well appreciated by the fishing community in Brighton. Sam the lobster man knows all about the scallop beds of the Seine and those early voyages to

Newfoundland returning laden with salt cod. On a short trip back to Brighton, we set off early one Saturday morning to bring in the lobsters. I was impressed by how organised the work was, hauling up the pots, returning the small catch to the sea, re-baiting and then launching the pots back over the side. Then on to the next stretch of rocky habitat favoured by crustaceans, a sonar panel in the wheelhouse keeping a watchful eye on the depth of the seabed. The waves were not particularly rough, but you got an idea of the potential for danger, the rocks, a snagged rope, a sudden change in the weather. The dark lobsters come glistening out of the water, their tails a little fan of inky blue with orange trimmings. After a while the colours lose their lustre, activity subsides and the claws are bound with rubber bands. They sit silently in their baskets, only a stray cuttlefish puffing away with indignation as if summoning the energy for one final burst of ink. In the cabin, the radar screen marks out a menacing bank of rain that somehow eludes us as we slip back inside the harbour walls. Bisque soup for Sunday lunch.

***

Got back to Rouen just as term breaks up, the students departing the house with glee. Students, not in the Brighton sense of nights on the town and days on the sofa, but young people who rise early, clock into lectures and return home to study some more. Now they are off, roof racks piled high, and the town has a real holiday feel to it, with open air theatre rock concerts and France progressing in the European Cup. I make for the quayside, exploring the chance of hitching a lift on a working barge, but there are no takers. No puffing chimney stacks or painted milk churns, these are barges with net curtains and big dogs to keep intruders out. I return once more to pedal power for the Westward journey down the Seine.

Early morning mist softens the industrial landscape. The dockyard silouette of silos and cranes tails away at Val de Haye, where a lone column with an eagle marks Napoleons' return from exile. The road wanders inland for a while before arriving at the crossing to La Bouille. A bright red gondola of a ferry draws you towards a village set beneath five rounded clifftops. On top of the hill is a fortified tower now converted into someone's home, the only ramshackle building on a riverbank of manicured finesse. Gradually the road climbs to a panorama of cliffs rising alternately on either bank and fields ebbing away to shades of straw. South of Duclair you are into serious fruit growing country, with apple, pear and plum trees and roadside stalls piled high with cherries. Another ferry carries you over to Jumièges, a pretty village with a wonderful ruined abbey. It is impressive because of its age, begun in the ninth century, and also its size. Two enormous towers at the front and a great wall behind, linked by naves and arches that retain a remarkable sense of unity. So much of the abbey stands intact, it would make a terrific backdrop to one of those 'son et lumière' spectaculars that light up the summers night.

A little further north you approach a magnificent modern bridge leading to Caudebec-en-Caux. Bands of steel stretching upto riverside towers, like two transparent pyramids suspended above the hillside. It is a long steep climb up the Pont de Brotonne, then a sweeping descent inside a barrier rail no higher than my handlebars. Got installed very reasonably at the Hotel St. Philippe, scrubbed, fed and seated at the bar in time for the European final. Not much can happen in a place like this, one square, a bridge and a prom, but when Trézeguet scored the golden goal, a procession of tricoloured cars took off to a pounding circuit of Abba anthems with a chorus line from the balconies. Around midnight the town went back to sleep but it had known its hour of glory.

The next morning I got up improbably early and wandered around the town. Caudebec centres on a lovely church with an imposing tower and a mass of coloured glass. La Sente de la Vignette takes you above the river and into a sunlit forest, and a few miles north a road leads through golden fields to the hamlet of Saint Gertrude. A little church, a water mill and a few peasants tending their patch, the Restaurant des Chasseurs is a wonderful location to take lunch. West of Caudebec on a loop in the river, is Villequier, home of the Musée Victor Hugo. More than a cottage but not quite a castle, it stands in a rose garden with statues and dinky outhouses you could spend all summer in as a child. Inside there is a billiard table with no pockets and an aquamarine beize. On the walls, several sketches by the author, one of a dark beguiling castle, the ancestral home of Cruella

154

DeVille. A tiny wooden staircase leads to a sequence of exquisite bedrooms that would reorient your life around sleep. I scoured the family tree for any trace of a Mûle lineage. Victor Hugo would probably have bequeathed this place to the orphaned and dispossessed of the world, but I want it for my own.

Over on the left bank is La Route des Chaumières, a quiet road of thatched cottages, some pristine, others settling like comfortable chairs into a form all of their own. At l'Eglise St. Martin a sailing ship and lifebelt hang inside the window, the walls etched with the thoughts of ancient mariners, a local feature known as pious grafitti. Here and there castle ruins break out of the ground marking the scene of long-lost battles. The Forêt de Brotonne descends the hillside, wrapping itself around the road, then retreats at Le Vieux Port to reveal a perfect village beside the Seine.

From the crest above Le Vieux Port, the end of the idyll is in sight. Port Jerome, chemical capital of France, a complex of nuclear domes, pressure cookers and bunsen burners flaring into the sky. Two chalk headlands rise in a final display of grandeur, before the river banks fan out to mudflats and lines of pylons marching towards the sea. I cut inland at Lillebonne where a powerful Roman ampitheatre, bedded in lush grass, embraces the little terrace of the Café du Théâtre. A winding lane follows the valley out of town, past a trout stream and a sign for foie gras. There was no one in at the farm, just geese clambering out of their tumbledown house, singing for their supper. I lay down on the verge, located

Foucart on the map and awaited the stopping train home.

***

One humid morning, the horizon strangely light beneath a menacing sky, the bell towers of Rouen shone like windows through the darkness. Steamy clouds devoured the dockyards, kettle drums rolled around the town, shards of witchcraft duelled with the cathedral spire and columns of rain riveted the road. Above my window the three resident pigeons looked out of their alcove and decided to stay indoors.

The storm was succeeded by days of sweeping skies, clouds clearing to gleaming sunlight before the next batallions gathered over Mont Saint Aignan. Immobilised from serious outdoor pursuits, I waited for word on the restaurant. The spirit of the kasbah held sway, one final offer succeeding another, but then out of the blue a price was agreed and the little place on the Rue Eau du Robec should soon be mine. I sat in the Café Curieux, looking round its ancient beams and jukebox, and wondered at life as an English chef in Rouen. Walking home, a display of fireworks took hold across the river. Trailers rising and falling with grace, shellfire breaking and bursting into smithereens, a fanfare spreading across the sky. The rehearsal for tomorrow, le quatorze juillet, when the Windsors stroke their necks and the clergy close their doors.

***

Back into the countryside to investigate supplies of food and drink. The Viking man with the barley pouch has his beer fermenting inside an old barn, with a mural of Nordic types sailing, partying and blowing their horns. His wife led me through a tasting of eight different beers, the best one 'la servoise', lightly infused with honey and heather. The Vikings know a man with an excellent goats cheese and he knows another who smokes salmon and trout. A network of possibilities turning in my mind shaping the content of a menu. I cycled to Buchy, sat in the shade of a bar tabac and enjoyed an Emmental omelette. Across the square a cattle auction was in full swing, the beasts parading to a measured commentary on their family history and favourite feeds. Then interest stiffened, Peter O'Sullivan took the mike and the bidding set off at a cracking pace. The deal done, the crowd broke with an emphatic shrug and proceeded with some purpose to the business of lunch.

At Buchy station I casually pushed my bike over the deserted tracks, and watched as an old lady selected to do it the hard way. She lugged a brute of a suitcase up and over the footbridge, losing a wheel on the way down. 'Not a station for the handicapped. I will have to write.' And undoubtedly she will. I have become accustomed to the little train that travels West to Rouen, two compartments and a bicycle van, it revs out of the station in a flourish of flag and whistle. On board, a big boxer suffering from the heat, face like an old fashioned football, exchanges a deep frown with its mistress and shares the rich flavour of its breath. The ticket inspector presents himself to the carriage, indulges in small talk, shifts a weighty tomb from one armpit to the other and rolls the door reassuringly shut.

That evening I ate at La Réverbère, the restaurant run by the Portugee and his wife, both of them called José. Madame relaxes the room with an easy maternal touch, the chef occasionally emerges from the kitchen, hangdog look masking a sense of mischief. Nothing quite surpassed the opening gambit of a smooth, delicate chicken liver mousse. Then there was sea trout in a reduced basil sauce, melting slices of foie gras and finally a caramelised millefeuille like crisp cushions of air. The macaroon with the coffee was worth the admission fee alone. I got home to discover ants besieging my window, not something you expect beneath the roof of a three storey house. The birds too have been behaving strangely, wheeling and screeching all the hours of daylight.

Something is a foot.

**

Ross, who has just made off to the Lebanon on a tandem, assures me that although modern cycle wear may look ridiculous, it provides a quality of buttock protection never before dreamt of. The first cycle shop I went to had shorts as tight as a tourniquet, and the second only stocked the full body harness, requiring a lycra leap of faith I was not prepared to make. So I pulled on my trusted baggy shorts and set off along the Seine on a day of scorchio sultriness.

Everyone must have made for the coast, because the pretty village of La Bouille was deserted and I was the only diner in a restaurant sheltering between cliff and river bank.

I climbed previously uncharted territory, the road rising steeply to the Château Robert le Diable. An old Viking vessel shelters inside the walls, a family of goats cropping the grass around the unique hilltop boathouse. All three castle towers are freely accessible, with striking views across the Seine and the industrial heartlands of Rouen. Down below, the dungeons portray scenes from Norman history, and there is a family tree of the first dozen Dukes of Normandy. Rollon the Viking begat Guillaume Longue Epée, then came Guillaume le Conquérant, Richard II, Henry Plantagenet and finally Richard Coeur de Lion. Robert le Magnifique originally founded the castle, but after an unfortunate encounter with pestilential serfs he was downgraded to Robert le Diable.

Plague makes a frequent appearance in these parts. In the basement of the Préfecture in Rouen there is a display of presses and pestles that were used for herbal remedies at the time of the Black Plague. I was at the Préfecture to obtain a residence permit, and was sent to wait in an airless room laden with despair. Thirty people were ahead of me in the queue, and I set down my earthenware pot and sank into a state of vacant waitfulness. Finally activity stirred out of the void, the buzzer surging into life, stopping just one short of my ticket number. I unlocked my lips in readiness to speak, and fearing paralysis from hours

159

in a bucket seat, limbered up ready for the summons. I did not exist for the pale functionary the other side of the bulletproof glass. He averted his eyes, talked to his desk, went away and came back only to conclude I was one document short of the full tally. Next time I will ride up with spiked mace and full chain mail, and claim my Diablesque rights.

Freewheeling down the castle hill did little to relieve the torrid heat, and it occurred to me there would be no better time to visit the cool, Troglodyte caves at Croisset. I crossed on the little ferry at Grand Quévilly and arrived at the Convent St. Barbe. In the fifteenth century Franciscan monks set about the Herculean task of carving out a monastery deep beneath the cliff face. There are dormitories, a kitchen, a well rising with the Seine, and a series of salt cellars extending far into the hillside. In the seventeenth century the stone excavated from the caves was used to build a more conventional church at the roadside, but the grottoes still provided a place of sanctuary. One wall carries an etching of a guillotine with a rolling head, and in 1944 the locals took to the caves to escape the blanket bombing. Today the Convent is a refuge for battered women. It has seen all the comings and goings on the river since Rouens' earliest days as a great port. In 1910 the explorer Commander Charcot sailed past en route to Antarctica, on a boat named 'Et Pourquoi pas?' I heard this phrase repeated in the pub the other night, and its crisp, rolling diction stayed in my mind. 'Et porquoi pas?' Because you will never return.

Strange to know days of hot summer in this region of dappled skies and sodden pasture. Rouen gone on extended leave, the shuttered streets left to tourists who turn their maps around and assume a look of learning aboard the miniature street train. Only the Sunday market is still bustling with locals, stalls piled high with scented orange fruit, chicken sellers roasting in front of their spits. George Bazins' biblical beard presides over ten varieties of goats cheese, one coated in powdery black cinder, an ancient form of preservation that precedes the use of salt.

Not all small producers will bear the cost of coming to Rouen. I was discussing this with the trout farmer when he called with a sample of smoked fish. 'Les paysans ont leurs habitudes', he said, standing at my window paring skin from a troublesome finger. The taste of the trout was altogether more delicate, gaining entry to a select list of products with the appelation 'Terroirs Normandie'. I noted a duck farm listed nearby and arranged to pay a visit. Just beyond the suburb of Bois Guillaume, the road meandered through harvested fields of wheat, arriving at La Ferme des Sources where a mule approached with a nodding welcome and a snowwhite baby goat. Inside the farm, everything duck beyond the beak. Duck sausages, terrines, magrets preserved in jelly and fatted livers of foie gras.

A few miles further West is the Château de Martainville with a scrunching gravel drive, lines of stables and a musty pigeon tower filled with gentle cooing. The castle is a beautiful building of wood and brick, four witch hat turrets flanking a pitched slate roof. A stone, spiral staircase takes you around the history of Norman crafts, rising to a ceiling like the wheel of a water mill. Each region of Haute Normandie has its own craft heritage, Le Pays Cauchoise to the North of the Seine, L'Eure to the South and Le Pays de Bray stradling the East. Martainville does not quite fit into any of these territories, but it is definitely part of Bovary country, a ten mile radius strewn with reference to Flauberts' famous book. Epicentre of le Pays Bovary is the Château Vascoeuil, until recently dilapidated and bound with ivy, but today a wonderful setting for exhibitions of art. The river Andelle flows through a park alive with sculpture, some bold and imposing, others figures of fun. This summer the castle was given over to paintings by Paul Aizpiri, wide-eyed modern minstrels set in striking colour.

On something of a castle roll, I made for the coast at Varengeville. The road west from Dieppe winds uphill, arriving at a spectacular view above Pourville, the sea sparkling and retreating to reveal an expansive arc of sandy beach. Down you plunge to a bright new esplanade with its own little oyster farm, then up once more over wooded cliffs to Varengeville-sur-mer. Les Dieppois have a long roll call of famous mariners, beginning with Jean Cousin who they claim discovered America before Columbus. Then comes Jehan Ango who in 1522 sent his own private flotilla to break the King of Portugal's control of the Atlantic sea. Ango built a magnificent château here at Varengeville, with a commanding view of his boats moored at Dieppe. The castle walls contain a beautiful domed dovecote, which at the time symbolised a 'seigneur' of absolute power. His name still features prominently around the port of Dieppe, but he actually died penniless following a war of attrition with the English.

At the other end of the village is Le Bois des Moutiers, designed one hundred years ago by Gerthrude Jekyll, a memorable name. The grounds begin in orderly fashion with pretty arches and peacock hedges, but the sculpted hand gives way to exotic undergrowth and enormous tree trunks towering into the sky. There is an unexpected feeling of space within the wood, space and soothing tranquillity, and you can sit for hours, burden lightened, becalmed above the sea.

***

Pale dawn crept through light mist, the hills emerging from slumber. The train pulled away from Monfort, a single track dot on the map, west on a line to Honfleur. After a spell of fruitless meander I found the River Risle and followed it from placid lake to rushing sluice gate, past cottages sprouting plants across the thatch, and a derelict church torn open by a thunderbolt, the graveyard still perfectly intact. I arrived at Pont Audemer veiled with dew, in need of a long infusion of coffee. Blue sky broke through the mist, and I set off around the town that once flowed with paper mills and barges laden with leather. Narrow lanes and waterways run either side of the high street, and tucked away is a beautiful park with an ornamental corner of wetlands. Up and over the hills, the real thing, the Marais Vernier, an expanse of lakes and luxuriant pasture that once formed a loop in the Seine. Today, as late summer sunshine took hold, maize plants faded given up on growth, and apples turned rosy on the tree. Stop to rest and there is nothing to hear beyond the chirping of birds and insects. Hard to imagine that fifty six years ago to the day, this region was liberated from the nazis, the countryside rolling over the scars and restoring a sense of peace.

I free wheeled around the marshlands all day, returning to the church at Pont Audemer, Medieval walls cascading with flowers. I retraced the river path and stopped at Condé-sur-Risle, a circuit of flies the only other sign of life inside the village bar. A wall of darts trophies, an Hungarian horse for sale and a poster for the weekend disco. Rural nightspots, a surprise feature of Norman life where carloads of youths converge from town to rhapsody till dawn. Got back to Montfort well before the train. Evening sun set the valley purring with golden warmth, the fields ascending towards a silouette of trees. Shadows encroached across the tracks and an oncoming light signalled time to go home.

Climbing the stairs I encountered The Hag and Lionel the artist on the way up. Invited in for a drink I was amazed at the transformation in The Hag; laughing, carefree, tutoying Lionel, plonking down her empty glass and swinging a leg in the air. Still suspicious that someone so malign could undergo a complete makeover, I escaped to the trill of my phone and Ros eager to impart that O'Kallaghans was bursting with beauties. Thence onto 'L'Opium' and the Mule stomping his hoof with the best of them. Nights and days of frenzy as the purchase date approaches. So much to do, suppliers to see, a team to recruit and the impasse of French bureaucracy to encounter. Madame la notaire, wide confidant eyes, finely honed fingernails, crystal clear content to her voice, guides me through the minefield. A series of signings where the maiden name of your mother is read out along with your marital status, broken, intact or 'celibataire', and amid much pounding of stamps a fee is paid always ending in a ridiculous number of centimes. Finally, as clusters of hazelnuts fall from the trees, I will join the procession down the hill each morning, tunneling into a world spelt winter and work.

Chapter 5

Cooking for the French

After all those lazy summer months of liberty, most of the day is now spent in a state of nervous excitement preparing for the opening of the restaurant. Just occasionally, dashing here and there, I catch an image which is all the more rich for its rarity. At the market, an archetypal peasant woman, headscarf and lined face, stoically playing Edith Piaf songs, a middle aged shopper swaying and singing in front of her. Just this morning, during a week of constant wind and rain, the sky cleared against the old tenement rooftops, pastel colours of pink and blue. And this evening, paid a visit to a dentist out of 2001 a Tooth Odyssey. Once through the second locked gate-o-phone, I entered into a reception area with massive Matisse prints and soothing water music, three television screens transmitting what both dentists and this scruffy intruder were upto. The attendant emerged with a Madonna Live headphone relaying information to the distant dental chamber, an incoming caller from the Planet amalgam and the computer terminal concerning the date of birth and hoofprint of Mister Mule. Enter a waiting room with this weeks' magazines, and was eventually summoned to the high tech studio, the young spaceman marvelling at the prehistoric nature of my English dental treatment. La France, number one in world football but also number one in healthcare.

I remember once laying prone with exhaustion, never wanting to get up, thinking had anyone told me of the trauma of starting a business, I would forever have remained a wage slave. And yet seven years later, I am voluntarily taking another turn in the tumble drier, this time in a country where every small transaction is a cactus-strewn obstacle course, banks are consumately incompetent, food suppliers reluctant to deliver for anything less than a lorry load, and a goodly proportion of the population are prejudiced against the idea of a foreigner setting up on their doorstep. After a catalogue of disasters involving an equipment supplier who should never again emerge from his serpents' nest, the opening day dawned, every fibre of the Mule in a state of tense frenzy. At one o'clock, the first customer emerged through a curtain of rain, only because the restaurant down the road was apparently FULL. She moused her way through the economy menu and a glass of tap water, and just when it seemed she would be the sole entry in the till, an emaciated woman tore across from the beauty institute opposite, and ordered a pot of tea. Thus was the pattern set for week one, a beginning beneath every expectation.

Two consecutive lunchtimes brought a sudden flurry of activity, but then the barometer fell once again, sweeping rain confining custom to sporadic ones and twos. October, it seems, is a bad month, doormats dented with tax demands, culminating in La Fête de Toussaint when France celebrates a day of death. Success measured in throwing away lettuce rather than poultry, but overall we are bumping along close to empty. We being me and my wonderful front of house find, Fouzia Babou, who is fun, understanding and has made the service area her own. Each day attired in a splendid new costume, sleek hips and plates casually poised all the way up her arm. When the sight of the empty restaurant is an onerous physical presence, she offers light-hearted relief.

I have just begun reading 'Madame Bovary', and have been entranced by the familiarity of the locations in the book. La Foire Saint Romain which pitches camp on the banks of the Rive Gauche each autumn, a wagon train of gold-plated caravans at the foot of the biggest funfair in Northern France. Croisset, the riverside home of Flaubert, its shaded garden profiled against the Seine. Vassonville, deep in apple country, site of Charles and Emma Bovarys' marriage, just a stones throw from Auffay where next July Vikki and Steve will also tie the knot, in an old farmhouse with a dormitory of 24 first world war beds, a night of passion as discrete as a burglar with a wrought iron leg. And La Rue Eau de Robec, now home to my little restaurant, in Flauberts' time inhabited by the dyers of Rouen, who used the river Robec to soak their fabrics, turning the waters red, white and blue. At the back of the book, a chorus of scholars have acclaimed Madame Bovary 'the first modern novel'. I was not at first clear what they meant by this, but by page 100 I have a pretty good idea; Flaubert is the founder of Despair. Life represented by a gloomy corridor with no escape, no prospect of turning into a sun-drenched room, the future sealed in darkness, suicide an enviable option. Today, with inky skies producing their daily deluge upon the Gothic Rouen landscape, two suited Africans sat down to eat with a long-faced white woman. Throughout the meal the woman irrigated her beak with a silent stream of tears. In Normandy we can all be Madame Bovary.

Returning home in late afternoon, a rare shaft of sunlight broke through, highlighting the mosaic of leaves hanging gamely from their trees. Everything cleansed and shining, purged of every trace of darkness. The sky set red against the cranes on the Seine, a huge cloud of dust rising from the flour mills, white industrial palls of smoke caught incandescent in the slanting sun. I ran down the hill, almost late for my appointment at the local barber. My little tuft just requires a quick going over with the Number 3 clipper, but this can be an inordinately uncomfortable experience. Not so with my local man, a shy, camp soul, clothed and coiffured out of the 1950's, who provides a gentle tour de force round the old cranium, a soothing escape from worldly worries.

***

19th of November, the Sunday market is besieged by pamphleteers prospecting for the local elections next March. A level of participation unknown in Britain, the main reason being that town halls in France know real power. The Number 3 in the Jospin government has just resigned so she can devote herself to the mayoral contest in Lille. Who to vote for? Well the incumbent socialists seem to do a pretty good job. A massive new sports complex, le Stade Saint Exupérey has just opened, light and bright, touching the stars. Next year a new line is scheduled for the Metro, a cheap, regular network, never known to kill anyone, the blue carriages announcing themselves with a friendly dong on the old tram bell. Every evening at the local station, they polish the marble and glass.

The great thing about Sunday market is that I can see what is available for the coming week. There is none of that pristine, flavourless, year round produce, things run according to season. Rhubarb won't be back till May, soft fruit and melons are only meant to be savoured in the sun. There are abundant cabbages, earthy carrots and cauliflowers, a great variety of potatoes, plenty to compose a veggie winter platter – I have decided that if I am going to go down, it will be cooking the things I like. An Arab stall, third alley from Monsieur Chèvre, has a terrific range of spices and herbs, always a fresh bunch of mint for the taboulleh salad. The stallholder is totally disinterested in the TV crew that is touting a sense of celebrity. The fishmonger from 'Le Chalut', mischievous wink and a bobble hat, is giving forth into a microphone homing in across a mountain of mussels.

That afternoon six of us took tea at the Hôtel de la Cathédrale. The food and drink not memorable, but the setting totally splendid; ancient beams, beautifully upholstered chairs, polite French couples whispering over their doilies. Tuesday night we're meeting for an evening of jazz at the station café; the ex-pat social calendar, more inclusive than anything I knew in Brighton.

Awoke the next morning to find the restaurant opposite burnt out. Never inundated with customers, a sign recently went up regretting the loss of credit card facilities, and now the door hangs dislocated and charred. As if responding to this stark symbol, the sixth week of the 'Moulin de Mule' saw a healthy upturn in activity. The seventh Monday was dead, but it gave me the chance to fly away to the Prefecture for a final attempt to obtain a 'carte de séjour'. By now the waiting room was quite familiar, the dispossessed of the French diaspora come to claim their birthright. The patient silence broken by a woman reduced to tears, convulsed and alone in her bucket seat. Surely this must all be a terrible mistake and really there is another corridor with a fasttrack, velvet suite for superior citizens of the European Community. But no, the hours crawl by, and I imagine my contretemps with the clerk when he sends me away for a sixth time for a document that does not exist. This is Kafka couchemar writ large, Joseph K metamorphosing into an insect, shaking his antennae dispassionately as he refuses to apply the treasured seal of the Prefecture to residency in the Gallic world.

The afternoon fades on a tide of drizzle, and I look down onto the courtyard and watch the functionaries fleeing their cosy nest, salaried and pensioned against anything dangerously alive. I am certain the shutters will be pulled at any minute, but no, after three hours and twenty minutes I am at the grill and the clerk is almost friendly, moving strange muscles in his face to produce the tight little smile of a tortoise. But what is this? I must return again, and queue for another eternity? No, no, he shook his head in light hearted jest. Merely to pick up your 'carte de séjour' valid for the next ten years. Tore down the staircase, whooping into the street. Ten years! No such thing has been granted in Rouen since the Canadians liberated the town. That tortoise must be on acid.

Oyster barrows are out in the street, a thankless task in this season of incessant monsoon. Cobbles gleaming, the countryside sinking, mad cows spinning in the mud, the thinking remainder of the herd marching in troupe to the Prefecture, banners borne between their horns, 'Give us grass to eat and the sun may shine once again'. Swung through the doors of O'Kallaghans bar, bearing six plump oysters. If the climate is indeed terminally destroyed, and the Seine sweeps all before it in a churning tidal wave, then this would be my favourite way to go. Snug warmth, oysters slowly savoured in a mouthful of Guiness, and in the best of all endings to the world, the aphrodisiac qualities of the crustacean put to lasting effect.

***

People walk by, shafting a penetrating stare into the restaurant, then move off at a swift pace, distancing themselves from the notion of carrot gâteau with wild mushroom sauce. Groups on the magical history tour stand on the pavement opposite, swivelling their heads to the top of the building to be enlightened on how each succeeding storey was built to overlap the previous one. Nodding and noting, they move on oblivious to the restaurant below. On Saturday afternoon I stood inside the L'église St. Patrice, looking up at the marvellous stained glass windows and exhorbitantly gilded lamps, a wonderful soothing place, finally opening its doors as part of the Christmas calendar. There are an infinite number of such treasures in Rouen hidden away behind lock and key. Once in a blue moon the chapel at the Lycée Corneille hosts a public concert revealing a domed ceiling of breathtaking splendour. One day, the pneumatic gates that seal off access to much of the Medieval town, will become equipped with a touch too much intelligence, spontaneously opening to reveal beautiful buildings and ornamental gardens, damsels watering their window boxes, net curtains falling carefree from their pointed hats. And why stop at property. Let the tightly closed Normans, so devastatingly described by Maupassant as mean and suspicious, open up their arms in an effusive display of warmth.

Monday off to the Hotel de Police on another bureaucratic summons, a catalogue of corridors that stretches beyond belief. Three bull dykes man the reception area, gruff layers of chin stroked with insouciant pride. Behind them, a display of waxwork dummies in uniform, uncannily resembling the gendarmes that occasionally batter their way through the swing doors, incapable of mastering the concept of swing. The Tussaud collection must be an integral part of the state apparatus, because a similar display graces the entrance to the Customs Building where I went to claim the alcohol license. Chief Sitting Bull exchanged my passport for a visitors card, and dispatched me to the fifth floor, Poste 2832. A plain clothed inspector welcomed me in; just a formality to make sure I was not using the restaurant to peddle drugs or launder money. I pleaded guilty on both counts. He sent a steady look over his half moon glasses, cracked his Byzantine computer into gear and asked the maiden name of my mother.

If he'd waited till the weekend he could have asked her in person. We stepped inside 'La Couronne', the oldest inn in Europe, three spacious salons, luxuriously upholstered armchairs, John Wayne and the Queen of Monaco signing their approval up the stairs, a place to lunch at leisure and in style, cloches lifted in unison around the table, a warm apple soufflé lasting long into the afternoon, rain falling horizontally in another world outside. Madame Maître D, a slight but powerful presence in a striking pink suit with a body assembled across the 20th century, legs remarkably trim, neck hewn out of the trenches and face shining like an antique doll. The New Year menu, promising exotic fare, crystal glass by candlelight and Pierre on the piano, looks too tempting to turn down.

***

Two months into the venture, and Fouzia Babou announces she will no longer be a part of it. The Mule surprisingly relieved as a multitude of small elements had combined to spell 'difficult'. Once a brand new tube of clingfilm that rolled and packaged flawlessly, now the plastic snared on the sharp, serrated tongue. Still it has been worth it if for the name alone, lifted from the original script of Jungle Book. Next up for the post of chief serveur, one Ludo, many years in the profession, composed and undemonstrative, extremes of expression not known to exceed a sort of quaffing of the cheeks and a modest smile.

The French have two words for miserly, 'radin' and 'avare', the 'r' crucial in each case, one rasping the other rolling contempt for the miserliness that is all around. If Normandy had its own patois there would be another twenty variations, because believe me they are a tight-fisted bunch. No offer, however generous, would be complete without the recipient asking, 'And can you do me a deal on price?' Today I went to the boulanger that supplies the restaurant and placed a decent sized order for Xmas chocolates, something not far short of 300 francs. Just before paying I pointed to a single chocolate and said I'd like one of them with my coffee. Anywhere else in the world they would have thrown it in for free, but here the little foil drum was weighed and measured down to the last centime. I was never aware of Brightonians being particularly carefree with their money, but compared with Normans they are positively reckless. I took coffee next door at Le Café de l'Époque, an old style hostelry with ancient prints of the neighbourhood and a magnificent clock chiming out the hour. The menu is traditional and virtually unchanging, but they have a loyal clientele who like it like that. It is up to me to develop a custom that wants something different. Preferably accompanied by a little alcohol. Today we had three tables for lunch, none venturing beyond an exhorbitant quarter litre of eau minérale.

In the summertime something happened – ill health, family crisis – which meant Yaya and Hassina were no longer in their Brasserie on the Boulevard de la Marne. I tried a couple of meals under the new regime, but it wasn't the same and the restaurant smelt of toilet cleaner. Imagine my delight when climbing the hill home, I glanced in to discover the original family restored, the three immaculate children all shiny cheeked after four months in the Algerian sun. Almost a sense of rejoicing as a couple of trusted customers resumed tenure of their bar stools, conversation about the weather pursued with sparkling interest. Ground my way through an offering of Arab petit fours and after an interminable round of 'Bonne Années', continued my ascent home and a luxurious siesta prior to the New Years' Eve festivities.

'La Couronne' proved too costly and we booked instead at 'La Casa', an African restaurant near the Croix de Pierre. Things strangely quiet at first, just three rastamen with beehive woolly hats, bending their knees to the music then stepping out onto the pavement, thumbs and forefingers poised for some serious smoking through the steamy window. Back inside, Madame Gary Glitter, metallic dress sense, electric black hair and space invader cheekbones, was soon floored by three punchy tureens, whisky and banana, ferocious ginger and a version of Bissap far more concussive than anything I remember in Amiens. Then all of a sudden a terrific assortment of people piled in. A disdainful Annie Lennox and her diminutive French mother. A debonair, faded nobleman, chiseled features and cocked back head of Kenneth Williams, cravate and bloated hooter grafted from John Gielgud. Two beautiful doe-eyed African children moving effortlessly to the music, identical in every respect apart from the colour of their shoes. And a powerfully ugly woman in a long padded coat, now discarded to reveal a light curtain number floating around tiers of tassled pyjama wear. One face to avoid when midnight struck. Our host, sporting a spanking new yellow shirt straight out of the wrapper, embraced us with his soft scented beard and ushered in great platters of food, crisp brochettes of giant gumba prawns, and a lamb and grain combination that was spicy without being hot. Limitless bottles of wine were effortlessly opened, a delightfully un-Norman experience to celebrate the new year.

***

People are everywhere going down with the lergy, emerging after a week prone among the pillows, pale faces hanging from dark eyes. I seem immune, eternal, marching down the hill each morning, pounding back up at night, the rain bouncing harmlessly off the umbrella. Until one night, little gremlins start investigating the passageways to my eardrum, and that secret springboard lodged inside the nose lining, launches into action. The two 's' least loved by mankind, snot and sewers, have now taken over my life. The one on overdrive, the other sending odours seeping into the restaurant. The first is surely surmountable, multiple squeezed lemons and a direct supply from the Andrex puppy, but the second is proving more difficult to diagnose. You would not believe how many pipes run vertically from Le Moulin de Mule to the nether regions below. Bonnefond the sewer expert suspended himself headlong into the abyss and came up with a plan of action. It is now up to plumber Brianchon to do the necessary, but he is constantly unobtainable, the months of rain that have saturated Northern Europe laying claim to his emergency services. At last the plumbers arrive, the trusted lieutenant who has worked for three generations of Brianchon and his black-toothed apprentice. A bit of welding here, a pipe inserted there, and the drain in the kitchen floor is glugging away contentedly. A good omen I hope, as primeval fumes are not conducive to a wholesome meal experience.

'Rouen Magazine' the town hall weekly, has just done a little piece on the restaurant, and luckily the journalist came round the day after surgery was conducted on the sewer. The Rouennais must crave statistics because the Magazine is full of them, graphs depicting the quality of air, progress on the new Metro line and the census of 3.4 million Normans; a sizeable Viking outpost. This week there was one statistic I could not believe, 10 tonnes of dog turd dropped on the streets of Rouen each week. Firstly, any resident would hazard 100 tonnes as nearer the mark, giant great 'crottins' capable of felling a horse, trodden up and down a rainswept street, stretcher bearers carrying the fallen to hospital. Secondly, no French statistic is credible without 23 grammes or centimetres stuck on the end. And surely noone this side of the foreign legion would volunteer for the job of weights and measurement. Lunar shell suit, industrial gloves and a shovel. Images of strife multiply. Farmers arrive at dawn at the Agriculture Department and blockade the entrance with bricks and mortar, their protest at BSE. Back at the town hall, bus drivers are encamped on hunger strike, demanding the return of their six 'camarades' sacked for torching a bus. Turbulent currents run close to the surface that strains to keep the show afloat.

At last though we can lift our eyes to the sky as

the clouds have cleared to leave an infinity of arctic blue, just the odd tracer of a plane, and then a rosy hew settling across the horizon at dusk. Today wisps of mist played with the spires and the dungeon tower, a fairyland Medieval setting, the sun burning through to highlight the red face and trousers of the Chagall fiddler perched on my wall, an improbable shaft of enlightenment. Just before noon, a Breton man came into the restaurant after exhaustive study of the menu, and said there was not enough vegetarian fodder. I explained that up to now demand had been minimal, and most people thought me crazed for offering so little meat. In Rennes, he said, there was great vegetarian choice, often organic, and you felt all the better for eating it. He sat down and ordered a fish starter and a chicken main course. The committed French vegetarian, like an English gourmet asking for steak tartare 'well done'.

***

The station forecourt is a bustling place, escalators ascending through tumbling water, busloads of students packed off to the 'Fac' on the hill, and La Rue Champs des Oiseaux, solid iron bridge rising above the hillside from which the Paris train emerges midst a screeching of brakes. A heavy duty landscape that owes nothing to the Nasdac Index. The side streets are pock-marked with lacklustre hotels, beds reinforced with plastic sheeting, but directly opposite the station is the Hôtel de Dieppe, a place of old-fashioned splendour. Immerse yourself in the luxurious snug interior, exquisite dining salons, vivid canvases and a bar Bertie Wooster would have made home. The soberly uniformed barman composes a giant tray of cocktails and nonchalantly carries it over to the gathering of expatriate anglais. Grenadin, curacao and menthe, colours normally offensive, are transposed into something sublime. Everything about the place exudes quality, only the lift is out of place. No black, concertina gates drawn open by a white gloved hand, but a grey little cell, room for just one madame clasping her dog like a purse.

The English contingent, generally well entrenched on the pub front, have established Sunday as a day of more varied pursuits. 'Billy Elliot' in sub-titles; lunch at Café Paul with a favourite mezzanine table to sit and watch the world and waiters twirl by ; and a visit to La Chapelle St. Louis, a tiny ancient theatre showing a Brecht 'cabaret noir'. It stands beneath the trees on the Place Rougemare, so named after the wave of blood that flowed from a terrible battle between Richard the Fearless and Othon Emperor of Germany. The event is inscribed on an old brick building with a pointed roof, and playful wooden sculptures gamboling about the timbers. The little theatre rises within ancient columns and frescoes, but the performance was unworthy of the setting. Terrible stilted acting and a great porpoise of a man plodding about the stage singing dolefully in the voice of a eunoch.

The evening was saved by the taste of a true

tagine. I have had two bad experiences in Rouen and Morocco, North African greasy spoons, but Hassina knows the slow, scenic route. Three hours ago she planted the tagine pot into the oven, and when the pixie shaped lid was removed at table, the lamb, artichoke hearts and meltingly soft vegetables effused an aroma to awaken the most concussed of taste buds. No fruit in her recipe, other than a beautifully braised tomato, but lots of delicate flavour. Good, simple food does abound in these parts. At the market this morning I bought a jar of honey from a hamlet near Dieppe. Opened the lid on a dark, molten nectar, the smell of animal stalls and hedgerows and a stunning, scorched taste that plumbed the depths.

***

The Café Metroploe is no more. Dignified, unchanging, an oasis of peace. Last night a huge crowd filled the place, falling out into the street, mutedly celebrating the passing of a grand age. Monsieur Olivier as ever arms astride the bar, watching amid the commotion. What will he do now the window on sixty five years of life has been whitewashed over? And what of the regulars? The local lycée students, mopeds lassooed to the terrace railing, magician scarves unwound, Citanes hanging through conversations like 1950's film stars. The coterie of small time businessmen gathered at the bar, regulating affairs of state, the florist, the tramp and Mister Mule, left incomprehending and in a state of grief. A place that was familiar, undemanding and comforting, now taken away.

The next day the local paper covered the closing night, alongside an obituary to Michel Gueret, who started out in the the Hôtel de Dieppe in 1940, and rose to become patron. Degrees of longevity that will never again be known, certainly not in the case of the little 'Moulin' that is struggling to survive its first year. So much is inexplicable about the trade, one day 24 happy customers effusive in praise, the next day none, as in zero. The disappointing factor is that not one of the umpteen acquaintances I had made in the neighbourhood prior to setting up shop, have set foot through the door. People who had always offered a fulsome handshake and 'Bon courage', now pass by as if the place did not exist. It is dangerous making generalisations about character, but here the fracture between appearance and reality is something almost tangible. The obligatory fanfare surrounding welcome and departure and the ernest exchanges inbetween have little bearing on what goes on inside the head.

Sunday, and with longer hours of daylight a chance to renew acquaintance with the countryside. Took the train to Yvetot capital of Le Pays Cauchoise, notable only for a circular church with a pink bell tower. Just a few miles away is the pretty village of Allouville with two charcuteries, no less than ten cultural societies and the oldest oak tree in Europe. Propped and a little the worse for wear, the tiled trunk rises towards the sky like the tin man in the Wizard of Oz. Two tiny alters have been carved into the tree, one slim-line opening at the base and another at the top of a winding staircase. The village café is full of oak memorabilia, with a cosy wood burning stove capable of holding you there for days. Make the effort to cross the road and dine at 'Le Vieux Normand'. An enormous seafood platter of crab, oysters and bulots, then the tenderest of duck; three courses and cheese for a tenner. Through the restaurant window, an enormous old barn in a state of terminal decay, a few tiles clinging to the rafters like scales on the carcass of a whale. Wandered off down the lanes, an effortless freewheeling day after months spent trudging through marshland.

A two week half term and Rouen almost desolate. Cafés and bakers shut down, but a wonderful crop of exhibitions to savour. Stunning black and white photography by a man named Plossu, two displays of modern Norman art, and an exhibition of graphics by Georges Braque. Chugged out on the Metro line to Grand Quévilly, a huge estate of powerful white architecture, and there in 'La Maison des Arts' were Braques' birds in flight. It seems he and Picasso were so close for a time they were unable to differentiate their work. All these little treasures in out of the way places, often better than the big displays trumpeted by the Town Hall. The offices of the French state are a strange amalgam, at times possessing a Stalinist take on reality, at others capable of dashing endeavour. Take the Channel crossing. The demise of the last ferry operator left Dieppe bereft of purpose, so the government of Upper Normandy stepped in, bought the English port of Newhaven and a handsome new boat, the Vera Sardinia, erstwhile gunrunner on the Sicilian coast, but now a more than respectable means of whisking me back to Brighton when the fiesta of French bank holidays begins in May. And should a certain commercial venture end in failure, there will at least be a decent sized vessel on which to conduct a dignified retreat. Champagne corks popping from the poop deck.

***

Besieged mentality. Have become prey to a succession of malevolent 'commercants' who circle the unsuspecting newcomer, home in to inflict a dose of villainy, and fly off to distant lairs beyond the reach of all telephonic communication. Always cordial verging on the obsequious, a duplicitous manner that masks the sting. I have this week filed three petitions at the Tribunal d'Instance, attempting to recoup 20,000 francs spent on broken goods and fantom services. None too hopeful of the outcome but at least the fightback has begun, hooves honed to a sharpness, attempting to take command of events.

Recently discovered a baker on the Rue Beauvoisine with excellent wholemeal bread, orange with honey and a wonderfully light sultana and nut. Returned the next day full of praise, but Madame, long lugubrious face and big bulbous eyes, shrugged in frustration. The Rouennais are too narrow to try something diferent. When her child is older she will de-camp to the Normandy countryside where people value quality produce. Suspicious of change, deficient in every dimension of warmth, the Rouennais seem at one with their misery. Weeks of cold rain have kept Spring at bay, the paper filled with pictures of dingies floating down High Streets, La Musée de la Marine bubbling under water. As a renewed onslaught culminates in a torrent of hailstones, babes whipped from their prams by the wind, one Rouennais will turn to another with a mixture of resignation and pride, and exchange the mantra, 'C'est la Normandie'.

***

There are certain formalities of conduct in France that are far removed from the casual blokiness of England. Enter a familiar café and you could face a full half hour of greetings and 'bises' on the cheek, a sort of social penance, before ever placing an order at the bar. It is crucial to log away every salutation because you are not allowed to greet someone twice in the same day. Offer a 'bise' over croissants in the morning and then again in a bar at night, and the head will swivel away with disdain, you are left embracing a void. Still more perplexing, the conundrum of whether to adress someone as 'tu' or 'vous'. Ten years of the French school curriculum must be spent explaining this one, but to the outsider it will forever remain a mystery. Blaze away mischievously, directing tu and vous at the same person, and their eyes will cloud over, plumes of cordite crackling from the ears as the brain approaches meltdown. Ross, who lived behind the Town Hall before cycling off to the Lebanon, had a neighbour who already hated him, mistaking him for a German. Each night she emptied her dustbin onto the bonnet of his car. Familiarly adressing the old lady as 'tu' powered her into an outer orbit of apoplexy from which there was no return. Quivering, bolt-eyed, circling the stars with a garland fashioned from fishbones.

The 'bise' should be a totally platonic affair, heads pirouetting harmlessly, but 'Mami' habituée of the Brasserie de la Marne, relishes the chance of contact with younger flesh. She will go on 'biseing' indefinitely until you duck away under the table, or deliver a deft butt to the head. Seventy three years old, valiant all-day drinker and a little the worse for wear, she recently ran aground outside the old folks home, keeled over and sank in a mist of Kronenbourg. Back at the Brasserie, four of the regulars were wrangling over the longest road in Rouen, Rue de Renard, Rue Saint Hilaire, it wound on endlessly. If you walked into a North Laines pub and debated the longest road in Brighton, the Justices would shut the place down. Greater fluency in French reveals most café conversation to be supremely banal. After the predictable entrée 'ça va?' 'ça va'; a chasm. They might be Champions of the world but they know nothing about football. It is just something that has strangely appeared, a ball, ZiZi and this bald headed goalkeeper. There is no heritage, no terrace tradition, no worthwhile football talk. Humour? doesn't feature. The weather? never changes. Inspiration? Camus and Aragon lived a long time ago.

One formality of French life has recently slipped

from view. Hitherto, Metro carriages always exhibited an exhaustive list of people deserving first claim to a seat. The old, blind, infirm, women carrying children, mutilés de la guerre, mutilés civils... Anyway, today I noticed that the traditional list had been replaced by the logo of a blob in a wheelchair. One French foible I secretly savoured lost to bland modernity.

***

The train glided along the valley of the River Scie, pink, white and red blossom shining in the sunlight. Off to discover the goat farm that supplies the restaurant with cheese. A wonderful product, best left till colonised with mould, the sagging shape finally sliced to reveal smooth white creaminess and an emphatic rich flavour. On a rare bright day, humid warmth rose from the verges, little lilac flowers straining from the nest. Sped downhill to the village of Bellencombre, a busy little junction of country life, a few terraced houses, a baker, charcutier and the Café des Amis.

Got diverted by a sign to the V1 missile site hidden away in the forest. The air was chill, the wind swelling in the trees, thick, concrete silos, fiercesome engineering and a rocket launcher pointing towards England. Coming back to the road, a procession of vintage motorbikes drew up, gathering at a clearing in the forest. The helmets peeled off to reveal worn faces, perhaps veterans of the war. Swept down through the Fôret Limousine, the floor a haze of bluebells. Emerged among fields no distance from La Ferme du Val de Bures. In one barn the baby goats, clambering, snow white, calling to be fed. Next door nanny goats curled up on the straw, and a few proud Billys, preening for the camera, horns in splendid shape. A river had recently erupted through the farm, and Madame Bazzin picked her way along the duckboards, seemingly accustomed to the intrusion of rushing water. Her neighbour had known nothing like it in fifty years. A biblical plague of rain. The yard harboured two gleaming charabancs, and across the impromptu river a tumbledown shack with another gaggle of goats. Perhaps I got it wrong at Auffay almost two years ago, drawn to the gleaming spires of the city like a Norman Jude the Obscure. Perhaps I should have stayed in the countryside to crop the rich grass, swish a lazy tail and shelter under the apple blossom.

Chapter 6

Past Masters

Today is Pentecost, the 32nd public holiday in May. Assumption, Ascension, vacation Redemption, nobody has been at work for a month. Set off through Bois Guillaume to Isneauville, and arrived just as the congregation were emerging from church for Sunday lunch. They were all of an age where everything becomes difficult, standing, tottering, stooping. They briefly congealed in the entrance to the restaurant before nodding momentum carried them over the threshold to table.

A few miles on, Quincampoix has some lovely thatched cottages and a petanque green framed by images from the blacksmith's forge. A cool, bright day, it was easy rolling countryside all the way to Morgny le Pommeraye. A tiny outpost with just one stopping train morning and night, the hall beside the station played host to an exhibition of local art, among them the watercolours of Michel LePetit. I first met Monsieur LePetit when he designed the Mule for the restaurant, and relations have evolved into an amiable routine. I address him in the manner of Robert de Niro, he replies in a sort of cockney French, gapes in fake astonishment, then laughs with a freedom rarely seen in these parts. The still life of a red mullet possessed his trademark gape.

As chance would have it, the day after Pentecost was a public holiday, so I took the train to the Cherry Festival at Vernon. Had lunch at the 'Café de France', sorrel salmon with a glass of Pouilly Fumé, and went off in pursuit of cherries. There was an amazing range of exhibits, Bayonne ham, rounds of sheeps cheese, wines to taste from Bordeaux and the Loire, puppies for sale, grandfather clocks, and a toy hospital where teddy could be mended in a day. There was no sign of Indonesian folk music or the waiters' race around town, but perhaps the promoters had got a little carried away. In the whole Fête de Cerises there was just one stall of cherries. It is worth returning to Vernon though, a surprise package of steel and glass melded with ancient stone. Sat opposite the town hall square, water falling from a damsels' urn emerging through a bearded face. A stream of sturdy Africans pounded through the café in ritual pursuit of the lottery. Perhaps they have greater need than most to escape. Vernon is ostensibly the quaint gateway to Monets' Garden, but since January fifty cars have been burnt out and the CRS have been called in. Visors and riot shields versus an army of lost teens.

A few bends further along the river you enter another world. The fifteenth century Moulin at Andé has been transformed into a salon of performing arts. On top of the 'meule', or grinding wheel, is a circular chaise longue designed for creative lolling. Downstairs the worlds' prettiest phone booth, little windows veiled with lace and a velvet cushion to sit on. In the grounds a theatre troupe thunders by with gallows and galloping horsemen. There is a diminutive concert hall where a shiny domed Tibetan bongs away at chimes and vases, caressing the air with sound. Up a steep walled pathway deep beneath the trees, a grander affair, chandeliers gilded with coloured ivy, two pianists and a page turner, dutiful, smiling and trill. Outside, high above the Seine, a potting shed built around treetrunks, pegs stacked with artists smocks and a battered cavalry helmet.

I returned through a succession of beautiful villages and then was back in alienation land. Val-de Reuil has no signposts as no one would want to go there. I cycled for half an hour around bleak deserted streets, trying to locate the station. A brutal concrete entrance hall with four young blacks impassive beside a throbbing pile of speakers. Back in Rouen, I made for O'Kallaghans and Barbaras' farewell drink. It is the end of the academic year and several of the Anglo-Celtic crowd are flying the coop. Barbara and I used to perch sipping gossip in the Hôtel de Dieppe, but now she is off to join her dad, king of the turf in County Louth.

***

Heat haze over Rouen, the inhabitants winkled out of their shells, shutters and net curtains flung aside, the sleep of ages falling from their eyes. The cartoon designer who lives above the restaurant believes a good long summer can de-Normandise the Rouennais, and certainly the sunshine has brought the cash register to life, the terrace a hubbub of conversation punctuated by uncorking wine. A stage has been set up beneath the Cathedral walls, musicians orchestrating a silent movie, 'Journal d'une fille perdue', a glowering tale of lost innocence. Midnight strikes, lights project onto the magnificent facade and the film rolls with dark intensity, expressive eyes on overdrive.

Saturday night and waves of sound lure me down to Place Boulingrin, normally a blighted car park at the mouth of the Metro line, but tonight a mass of coloured smoke, toddlers swaying on shoulder back, the crowd responding to every entreaty to wave, chant or pogo on their heads. The band 'Manau' has hornpipes, fiddle and accordion, a Breton take on rock. Just the precursor to Midsummer night, when music takes centre stage in France. Classical repetoire during the day, the city orchestra playing Beethoven in the park, and an eight year old clarinetist on a bridge over the Robec, performing with consummate ease. By evening the streets come alive with bands, one sets up on the restaurant terrace and is off on a heavy metal bender. Walking home, the square outside O'Kallaghans is packed, Rose mounting the stage, capturing the crowd and 'Killing me softly' with style.

And the fun goes on. This weekend there is Medieval jousting on the castle walls at Les Andelys, Viking madness at the brewing farm, and a pyrotechnic bonfire on the Grand'Mare estate.

Decided to give the latter a miss as Grand'Mare is a forgotten enclave on the hill, where acts of arson are the currency of everyday life. You approach through leafy Bihorel and then suddenly the roads are potholed, windows boarded over and tower blocks rise above a forest floor more metallic needle than pine. Finally plumped for 'Viva Cité', a carnival of street theatre on the other side of town. The fusion of the concepts 'French' and 'Humour' should have rung a warning bell, as a pitiful number of acts faded into the twilight, jugglers who couldn't juggle, and a foursome who emerged from igloos to indulge in cryptic danse. The next day, the peacocks at Cléres made full amends, whooping in the woods then emerging in unison to fan their plumage, a quivering splendour of aquamarine. On either side of the château a choir and brass band played, the notes circling the pink flamingo lake and shimmering in the trees.

***

I encounter a wide mix of beggars on my way to work. At the bottom of the hill a blind man danses among the traffic shaking a plastic cup. Call me a cynic but I question the validity of his white stick. Once I hurtled towards him, brakes in disarray, and he stepped aside with the nonchalant ease of a matador. For much of the past decade he has worn the same hideously stained coat, weighed down by years of crusted dirt, but last week he appeared in a brand new beige number and coquettish baseball cap.

Perhaps I just do not understand Post-Modern man, but I expect my beggars grimy and toothless, not dressed by Jean Paul Gaultier. Under the subway and down towards town there is reassuring evidence of the old time dosser. Staggering towards you like a prolapsed cowboy, he spends his days in the garden d'Antiquités, irrigating the statues and watching the world go by. Just today I witnessed Gallic C Nesbitt roll to the ground in front of the restaurant, take a last drag from his cigarette and then defuse quite still. The wife of the architect rushed out to administer a final act of kindness, but her fussing restored him to cantankerous life, and he was upright as a crab, off to the corner café to scrounge a drink and a fag.

After lunch I like to relax on the terrace, modestly proprietorial in my blue canvas chair. A little terrier hops by carrying a lame paw, and an old dear ambles out in her slippers, legs in a terrible state. A rainbow coloured camper unloads a tattooed eco-warrior in leather shorts and vest. Unlike the French to be under-dressed. If they set out in matching waistcoat, jacket and chiffon scarf that is how they will stay, even when the tarmac is melting, the Seine steaming, birds turning monkey in the trees. The little train tootles by, not the usual cargo of solemn tourists anxious for it all to end, but a swaying flotilla of schoolkids exultant in song. Children do not greatly feature in the life of the Mule, strange blobs cosseted in three wheel drive prams, whining discontents, hyperactive wells of anxiety reducing parental life to rubble. But this rocking convoy had a sense of Brighton about it. Time to set the oven and bake the scones.

***

Alarm at Barentin station. The door to the cycle van was locked and I had visions of being marooned on the platform as the bike sped off to Le Havre. Two ticket collectors climbed down from behind the engine, sprinted along in their fine grey suits and scolded me for holding up the train. I adjusted my mask and pointy black hat, levelled a blunderbuss at their heads and made off with the mailbags.

Barentin is an attractive little town, with a viaduct spanning the valley, an impressive church set against the hillside and two modern statues in the old style, a knight slaying a red dragon and an Adonis awaking from slumber. An old industrial mill stretches along the banks of a stream, zigzag rooves, dark shattered window panes, and a great brick chimney stack. The whole complex is bordered by beautiful terrace housing with little latch gates and flowers hanging from the windows. No distance away at Villiers a banner announced a 'fête' this very day, but the street was as quiet as the little one track road that rose through wooded hillsides to St. Pierre de Varengeville, where an insurance company has set up home in an exceedingly grand château.

The sky darkened and the valley of the Seine filled with crackling thunder. Lodged in my childhood memory is the loss of John White, star of the Spurs Double team, struck by lightning as he sheltered under a tree. A flashing bolt of lightning exploded directly ahead, and I sped downhill to St. Martin de Boscherville, finding sanctuary beneath the awning of a barn. Two local lads joined me there, and they immediately knew I was English. My accent is terrible. A lot of it boils down to pronounciation of the letter 'R'. Take the RER, the urban railway that connects Gare St. Lazare with the Stade de France and the hinterlands of Paris. In French RER becomes a rolling rictus of catarrh, 'ehhrrghh eh ehhrrghh'. Rouen suffers similarly, absolutely no 'R' just a rasp of the throat ending in something nasal. Anyway, St. Martin de Boscherville has a magnificent Abbey, all the stones freshly scrubbed, just one dark corner coloured red with fading frescoes. Up above there is a sparkling organ, and the majesty carries on outside with immaculate outhouses and a terraced garden within Medieval walls.

Climbing the hill east, I stopped to savour the panorama of the Abbey nestling in an expanse of pastureland. Another downpour broke from a blue sky and I sheltered in the Fôret Roumare, steam rising from the pounding earth. Then downhill to Maromme, a huge encampment on the outskirts of Rouen. There is an apochryphal tale that one Caesar or another, arriving at this spot beneath five hills, named it 'Ma Rome'. The spectacular hillsides give rise to tower blocks, connected by a brand new tramway to the centre of town. A potent symbol of public spending that may now be at an end. A new tax cutting mayor has emerged, Pierre Albertini, casting a sidelong lizard look over the town.

Not far away, Notre Dame de Bondeville has a quite exceptional museum. Once a textile mill on the little river Cailly, it has been transformed into La Musée de la Corderie Vallois. Many of the old mills in Normandy are still and silent affairs, but this one has an enormous wheel ploughing the water like a Tennessee steamboat. The paths are ornamentally overgrown and you enter beneath a gleaming copper walkway, bobbins and spindles dancing and turning, driven on by an English engine. The foremans' office has been carefully recreated with a sepia diary, a tube of pastilles opened on the desk, and a list of dyeing instructions. Upstairs, a separate exhibition celebrates a century of cinema. More spools and spindles, magic lanterns and matinée posters from the past.

Currently showing at La Musée d'Antiqités, 'Iron Age 2', a tale of Druid ritual and sacrifice from Caesars 'War of the Gauls'. Excavations at Bois Guillaume, close to my hilltop nest, have produced new pieces of pottery and strenuously forged wheels. There are two enormous mosaics, one sunken like a Roman bath, another embracing a wall. The permanent exhibition has a lovely quadrangle of arches with faceless statues, coloured glass, and the beams that supported old Rouen. One portrays scenes of a voyage to Brazil, Normans puffed out in hats and jackets, natives lithe and bare. Two magnificent stags rise in farewell on the stairs, then you're out across the yard reserved for La Société des Savants, into Rue

Beauvoisine, where the image of a craftsman, stooping and still, is preserved in the clockmenders shop.

Heritage is everywhere. Just today I read in the paper about three different lives dedicated to the past. Jacques Montier built an old style carousel outside his house, hand-carved horses chivvied along by Romany flutes and cymbals. Jean-Jacques Falher turned his farm into a museum of early crafts, the making of cheese, bread, barrels and lace, thousands of objects that died with their owners now restored to life. Pascal Gilles left his job as a delivery man to learn the blacksmiths' art. He now shoes horses for fifty kilometres around, assiduous in cleaning the foot beneath the hoof. 'It is absolutely essential that the animal feels good.'

Made a note of his number.

***

The train edged out of Rouen, past two industrial workshops hewn out of the rock, 'Lampisterie' and 'Exploitation'. A taxi, primed at Dieppe, got me to the boat just in time for a weekend back in Brighton. Hoverspeed, cowboys of the Southern Seas, have taken their service concept from the fairground House of Horror. You settle into a corner of a little compartment that sets off sedately, before crashing through the harbour gates into the wild beyond. Eyelids close down on darkness, a fragile veil of protection torn through by searing shocks. A gust of vomit scorches the nostrils followed by a hot flannel in the face, courtesy of a grinning mannekin in a pagegirl suit. A heffer with elephantitis tumbles into your lap, one of the procession of grotesques compelled to circuit the sloping walkways, dayglo shell suits, sawn off leggings, socks on sandalled feet. White noise spirals from a wall of one arm bandits, industrial handriers blast through the toilet door, arid laughter, conversation too inane to be true and a tide of infant rebellion rising to a spasm of febrile lungs. Just when you are conjuring visions of a celestial Eurostar capsule, the hovercraft breaks into the clear daylight of Newhaven harbour, lines of seagulls waving from the cliffs, the Fellini cast slipping away, never to emerge again.

A Connex pony express canters round the corner, falls lame at Lewes but soldiers bravely on to Brighton, a town more electrically charged than ever. Fat Boy Slim has just performed on the beach to a cast of thousands, and every vacant tarot card den is being turned into cocktail, sushi madness. The only person in town with little to sell is Carol, the wind having kept the trawler at bay, so I pulled out a sunlounger beside her barrow and traded news through my floppy blue hat. That night ate excellent fish at The Regency opposite the West Pier. Then up Dyke Road to visit Madge, fifty years married to Charlie, the oldest waiter in town. A Barnados boy apprenticed to the Eastbourne Grand, he served at Dunkirk, Burma and the Normandy Landings, before forty years working the smartest hotels in town. Well into his seventies he still held court in Burgundy jacket and bow tie, flirtatious eye for the ladies and a brush off for the gents. Half deaf, dodgy ticker, unsteady on his pins, he would transform an order for Spotted Dick into a script from Carry on Crumble. Last November he passed away and Madge is left with her dolls and the memories she recounted over a bottle of Bergerac wine.

Refuelled with human warmth, I returned on the early boat which stalled mid-Channel, struggling into Dieppe on half an engine and a handrier. Made straight for my kitchen and the whisking of one hundred chocolate genoese, preperation for the most celebrated wedding in northern France. Vikki and Steve are friends to savour, and the posting of the Banns lit paths from Ireland, Scotland, The Lebanon and Spain, a gathering of the clan of emigré Rouennais. Civic nuptials at l'Hôtel de Ville, lunch at Le Moulin de Mule, then onto Saint Maclou for the fully fledged ceremonial. That evening the whole troupe de-camped to a great barn near Auffay, a feast of foie gras, magret de canard, a stunning Calvados sorbet and champagne cascading through crystal glass.

The next day I returned to Auffay, canoes for hire and two metal drummer boys beating time on the church wall. Faded lettering outside the café revealed something of a grander past, 'Hostellerie de la Vallée de la Scie', spinning carriage wheels scrunching to the door, platters of game, cinnamon apples and foaming goblets of cider. Behind the café, a lovely park cut through with rushing water, and the tiniest toilet perched like a sentry box above a stream. A few miles away, the Château Le Bosmelet has fallen on hard times, the family silver being auctioned off in a marquee on the lawn, attentive faces, boater hats and crumpled summer jackets. Took a turn around the grounds. A path telescoping through trees to the silouette of a boy on a bike, the obligatory modern sculpture sprouting from the grass, and the roof of the gatehouse, a rolling patchwork of litchens and slate.

The succeeding week filled with insufferable heat, days of languid torpor, nights too dense to sleep. An orange half moon sat serenely in the sky, while a storm in the south flashed and rumbled like shellfire. On Sunday made a bee line for Pourville beach, simmering shallows, eddying sand and the embrace of a still sea. A few lazy strokes towards a lost horizon, then floating back to crumbling cliffs scorched terraccotta from the kiln. This is where Camus' Meursault killed the arab, beneath a blinding sky and a relentless sun. Somehow made it over the hill to Dieppe, and sat in the shadow of the Rue Haut Pas outside the Café de l'Union. One of the tenements has a tree filling the walls, another has crumbled into the street. The café clientèle have known better times, but Madame has undergone an upgrading. Robe filled with poise, trim auburn coiffure, and Dame Edna glasses exchanged for something softer. Her assistant remains unreconstructed Madge, wan face, goosey waddle and an apron born in the Crimea.

Returned on the train opposite an old man sucking a boiled sweet with the look of a baffled baby. Cloud cover settled over the city, the lid upon the cauldron, and I ate outside 'L'Orangerie' in the strange nocturnal heat. Langoustine quenelles, meaty mussels and mascapone ice cream melting into roasted figginess. All for a price which in England would get you tired pizza and tiramasu. How does a restaurant make a living over here? I do not know. The month of June every lunchtime was busy, yet I barely broke even. One week after launching the business, the African who owns the Baobab Tree looked me long in the eye and spoke in measured tones; 'You must never. Employ. Anybody'. The social charges will kill you. A month later, Philippe from the Bistro searched for words that could express the dead hand of the French state. 'On vous broye,' escaped through clenched teeth. 'They crush you.' Dip a toe into the black economy and you are dead. The thought police descend on a fishing fleet at 3 o'clock in the morning, a factory will be surrounded, exits locked, while they search for 'illegal' labour. If the millions of British shopkeepers took a look this side of the Channel, they would tapdance all the way home.

'L'Orangerie' was the town hall in eighteenth century Rouen, a cavern of criss-cross arches behind La Maison Pierre Corneille. Corneilles' country house has been turned into a market garden of his time. Follow the Seine past the silent Pulqué, cross on the ferry to Petit Couronne, and there it stands, wood and slate walls among ornamental borders. Lines of battavia, frisée and escarole, Milanese cabbage, medicinal plants and all the kitchen herbs we use today. Saffron comes as an exotic surprise, as does parsnip, no longer valued in these parts. They don't know what they're missing.

A history of local food, 'A la fortune du pot', has been assembled at Pont l'Évêque. Vineyards were common in the Middle Ages, Henry IV musing how such beautiful grapes could make so terrible a wine. Travellers to the East brought back artichokes, cauliflower and rhubarb, the origins of Madame Dufrennes' success. On 28th August 1563, a banquet was held in honour of Catherine de Medici, a significant event as her marriage to the king introduced Italian cooking to France. Flax has long been cultivated around the magical name of Doudeville. Originally bound with straw and clay to insulate the farmhouse, it has recently evolved into a healthfood; flax bread and flax pâté, full of the oils that make for a happy heart. All very remarkable in this land dripping with fat. Beurre d'Isigny is considered the best butter in the world and meltingly ripe Pont l'Évêque cheese is a wicked cholesterol treat. A dozen charcuterie windows hang with long fat sausage, one displaying the Lonsdale belt, 'Champion du monde des Tripes'.

The high street at Pont l'Évêque has grown organically out of the land, cows grazing to the left, a saddle shop to the right. The church has been seemlessly rebuilt, windows bright swirls of colour, unblemished by pious saints. The outer walls read like a roll call of modern warfare. Perot, Seventh Hussars, killed at Wagram, 1809. Tesson, lost on the retreat from Moscow. The terrible culling of the first world war and the 'victimes civiles' of the second. A park has been dedicated to Jean Bureau, mayor from 1939-1944 and 1953-1977. What caused his post-war fall from grace and why did they forgive him? Pedalled uphill to Beaumont en Auge, a living replica of the past offering a sense of identity. The priory founded by Bertrand, Baron et Vicomte de Roncheville, has a garden overlooking Calvados country, Caen, Bayeux and Mont St. Michel, signposts for a future tale.

***

I often saunter into the skylit ampitheatre at the front of the Musée des Beaux Arts, to savour the enormous splashes of colour by Raoul Dufy and the wonderful statues waltzing round the room. Last Saturday the place was filled with canapés and kir glasses, a gathering of the artistic élite come to celebrate a new exhibition, 'Romantics of the North'. Intense clusters gasped with excitement and occasionally broke into applause as expert curators expounded on the secret merits of each little print. A more drab and anaemic collection I have yet to see.

October is Festival time in Normandy, the French National Orchestra performing Stravinskys' Rites of

Spring. All tickets were gone the day they came on sale, but I went along with Mathilde on the chance of returns at the door. The entrance to the theatre was a parade of exotic plumage, costumes plucked from the catwalk, a strained sense of excitement, laughter cascading, in the words of James Baldwin, 'like a black fountain'. We were turned away from the ticket office empty handed, Mathilde, solid communist origins from seafaring Dieppe, decrying the bourgeoisie not for their wealth but their arrogance. The next night the Chapel Carmel at Bois Guillaume hosted a concert in a hall lined with unyielding seats. Burhan Öcal played the Turkish mandolin and a bongo drum with the flight, power and caress of enchanted hands. Black clothes, deep mullah voice, eyes fixed in the distance as though the audience were imposing on a private grief. Pascal Conteh breathed life into his accordeon, an extension of himself. His first piece began with a window creaking in a gale, the storm unfolding then diminishing to the same unresolved pane. Then the Turk and the Frenchman played off each other in a remarkable symbiosis of their two traditions. The rows of solid Normans beat their hands in a crescendo of acclaim. We had witnessed something special.

Autumn and piles of mushrooms appear at market. Girolles, pinheads on gangly stalks and little in the way of flavour. Charcoal black trompettes de mort, and ceps, big brown caps on broad trunks, moist and yielding with a smell that can only be described as sexual. This weekend more than fifty local producers set up in the Rue Rollon for the annual 'Fête du Ventre', a celebration of authentic fodder. Prime attraction were the flax farmers from Doudeville, dressed in ancient peasant gear and given to impromptu bursts of chanting. This seemed to mesmerise the Rouennais who eventually cast caution to the winds and piled in for a taste of flax bread and cookies. Both distictly nutty.

Rue Rollon leads to the Place du Vieux Marché which for centuries teemed with everything food and drink, Corneille threading a path through the crowd, barrels of cider and salt cod, a commotion of buying and selling right in the heart of town. The municipal market held sway until the 1960's when it was moved to a cluster of hangars near the docks, and replaced by the l'église Jeanne d'Arc. Roof like the tail of a diving whale, a spire running horizontally across the square like some fantastic creature from the sea. The ebb and flow of a vibrant market given way to a place of silence, the surrounding hostelries cleansed and historified to cater for the tourist crowds.

Stepped inside the Brasserie de la Marne to find the regulars slowly turning in fond embrace, entranced by the sounds of Radio Nostalgie. Toothless men, painted ladies, flotsam that have been pounded on the shore, risen up and holding on for all they are worth. Ate my couscous beside a genial old Arab, eyes sparkling above a babble of senseless conversation. Rounded the corner to l'Hôtel de Dieppe to indulge my newfound passion for

Benedictine, the smooth golden liqueur distilled for centuries at Fécamp monastery. Through into the dining room, the Maitre D was dissecting a grilled duck with the graphic clarity of a silent movie actor. Once the breast and thighs had been removed, the commis crushed the carcass inside a gleaming copper vice, and returned the juices to the maestro for incorporation into his flaming sauce. Canard à la Rouennais.

Less sophisticated, a primal treat, is dinner at 'L'Ours Noir'. The smell of pig roasting on burning wood draws you to the makeshift restaurant at the Foire St. Romain, encamped on the left bank of the river. The doorman, something of a beast himself, pork pie hat, thick dark coat, jowls like Fred Flinstone, eventually swishes a tail and you are in out of the cold, inside a huge marquee with hundreds of people tucking into oysters and the prized cochon du lait. Flesh exceedingly tender, crackling crisp and chewable, portions fit for a return from the Crusades. The big dipper after a pig supper proved an unwise choice, so I settled for a gentle turn on the ferris wheel. Up and up it rose towards the Cathedral illuminated on the opposite bank, then down through the night, the city of Rouen fading away.

***

The Hag has been a benign presence lately, labouring tirelessly in the little garden, perching huge pots of geraniums on the window sills and rushing out to bring them in when wind or frost threaten. Yesterday she caught me on the stairwell with renewed evidence of the bizarre manias that fill her mundane life. Had I been disturbed by the excessive heating the previous night, registered at 27c inside her coven, impelling her to throw open her shutters to the starry night and sleep stark naked on the tiled floor. Every now and then she intersperses her ramblings with comments of an unexpectedly sexual nature. Late one evening I had just put the bike to bed in the cellar, when she appeared on the stairs in her nightware, long hair unleashed about her like a Medieval crone, 'Oh monsieur, I thought there was an intruder,' she grinned toothlessly, draping herself backwards against the bannister. Then once when explaining how to operate the tricky key to 'la salle technique', the dark cupboard where she keeps a goodly supply of iron age implements and a very long hose, she slipped the key inside the hole, engaged the inner mechanism and breathed faintly, 'et voilà, it works just like a woman'.

For all her frailties the Hag ranks second for social contact behind the artist in the attic. Then come the two ancients who inhabit the basement flat, one confined almost permanently to his bed, the other still capable of staggering out to the letter box each day, nodding contentedly against the wall on days of unblemished sunshine. The remaining dozen inhabitants of the house turn the double locks behind their doors and select a life of exclusion.

One hundred years ago a cartoonist depicted Rouen as a giant chamber pot. Clouds funneling between the hills along the Seine, sealing in the fumes from the factories and dousing the inhabitants with rain. Down in the bowels of the chamberpot, furrowed faces struggled to hold onto their brollies in the teeth of a turbulent squall. Some cities suffer from outdated images; the caricature of Brighton as a seedy, sticky piece of rock has 'lazy journalist' written through the centre of every tale. But Rouen deserves its chamberpot status. Three times a day the streets are heavy with the sound of Gothic bells, muffling carefree laughter, a whistling song, smiles diminished to the opening and closing of a cat flap. There is the occasional chink in the darkness. Manu who lives next door to the restaurant is a beacon of happiness, with an insatiable appetite for nightlife, but he was not born a Rouennais. Cristophe and Natasha, successors to Monsieur Olivier at the 'Metropole', raise their heads from the perpetual round of service to offer a welcome, sound as the marble columns of the café. And there is 'Le Buro', a little gem of a bar on the Rue Ecuyère, where Rémy composes extravagant cocktails, hoisting them through the throng on a luminous pink tray. The regulars, a combination of youthful and faded elegance, wrap you into their entourage producing an unfamiliar sensation of warmth. Outside, the mainstream brigade scuttle along headown, tame and timorous, feeding into a shifting sands mentality that carries something from a Vichy past. When the Canadians crossed the Seine at Elbeuf to liberate Rouen on 31st August

1944, the Mayor René Stackler was described as 'non-résistant mais non-adversaire des résistants'. What exactly was he then??

The restaurant, like the people here, is just struggling to get by. More than one voice has questioned the wisdom of setting up something even mildly veggie in a place so resolutely carnivore. At a time when new cases of French mad cows surpassed the numbers in Britain, it did not seem outrageous to believe that the 13th largest city in France might sustain just one little légume restaurant. Hélas, I have been aware of only a single genuine vegetarian, who travels in monthly from Oissel, ten miles down the river. Arriving at Oissel station after a ride through the Forest of Rouvray, I wandered off to capture a picture of clouds reflected in a puddle on the platform, turned round and my bike was gone. I do not share the local prediliction for life as synonymous with suffering. It is time to saddle up and go.

***

The Transmanche ferry had an inauspicious beginning, arriving mid-summer forlorn on the quayside, not even the Tourist Office at Dieppe could tell you the times it set to sea. But now the Hovercraft no longer bounces along like a duty free dustbin lid, Vera Sardinia has come of age. Tons of open deckspace leading to the Ponti di Commando, where a leisurely captain in wrap around shades ushers the vessel out to sea. No mall, no musak, nothing remotely modern, just old fashioned prices in the dining room with a wide angle view of deck and sea. Dirk Bogarde in his bathchair, casts a shipwrecked eye over the matelots, a wave of Mahler strings pitching and falling away. Images of a town emerge on the shore, Sidney Seagull, Stomp City, the Albion risen from the ashes, steep hillsides of brightly painted faces, streets alive at night, a few pearly fishermen mending nets on the beach, simple values like the past.

Hello Vera, you lovely old tub, carry The Mule back home.

Chapter 7

A Mule in Brighton

Last shift in the kitchen of the gargantuan Fat Fryer. Everything gets thrown in, sausages, eggs, frisée lettuce, its foaming presence coating every surface in nicotined stickiness. My prospective replacement began the day in studious silence, but like any onetime Kitchen Porter, could not resist loquacious flights of fantasy. The houseboat he's about to buy with diamond studded slim-line tele, DJ decks, solar panels and a wind generator turning among handsomely painted milk churns, the icing on the cake that will one day glide across the Channel and penetrate the Continent. What is it about kitchen porters that gives them such a warped take on life? Years of sink vapours inducing Trench Foot of the brain.

At Michel's Brasserie in Oxford, the KP rolled up to work in a stetson. Occasionally he would be dispatched to the cellar to sew mailbags and peel vegetables. He always emerged with a mutant carrot swollen like a giant genital. One day when I was racing down for some frogs legs from the freezer, I heard him whisper,'I can see right up your skirts', which was odd as I was attired in regulation check trouserware. Decided not to tarry and torpedoed back upstairs.

The gauleiter proprietor of the fat fryer produced the odd nugget of Huddersfied humour, but was more consistently adept at demolishing kitchen morale. She admonished the Mule for an incorrect garnish on a burger, and cast black looks over any moments of repose. I began to look about for a dinky little eaterie still at an affordable price. An opening in the North Laines sent me off to the town hall in search of planning rites. Someone has tried to update the image of civic staff by clothing them in uniform that was surplus stock in the Gulag. The planning advisor arrived, grey green tunic hopelessly crumpled, voice thin, dry and cadaverous. He pressed the maps close to his face, on the one hand and the othered, and strange to tell at the end of it all, no definitive advice had been offered.

But no matter. Left to hover in a vacuum in time, things could not be more pleasant. Days of blue sky, idle gossip, the occasional dip in the sea. A dog like idyll of food, slumber and mischievously breaking wind. On Saturday, all reserves of sleep evidently exhausted, I awoke with the dawn and decided on a day of real activity. Took the bus to Lewes prison where Billy Mule once made me pottery and a bear inbetween classes on the computer. I said it was like a holiday camp, but really dreaded the cold stone walls, the clanging of giant keys, and knew I could not have survived a solitary night. At Lewes Billy was a hero. Took the bridleway that skirts the prison walls, up past the stud farm with a row of stables each topped with a little flat. Higher still to Mount Harry and the Black Cap which look out onto the whole world, lines of hilltops running this way and that, fields folding like waves down to the distant glow of the sea. No sound other than the wind in the leaves, gathering the clouds, and the onward plod of each hoof.

Summer broke in spectacular fashion, a wild storm tearing down trees and traffic lights, just the fragile little plants in my garden embracing the deluge with glee. Sat eating bangers and mash in one of the swish gay bars that now colonise Marine Parade, impassively absorbing the maelstrom of the sea. A couple in macs and rain hats stared in at the window, silently weighing the options of refuge among 'topless barmen' or an imminent watery grave. I bit the top off a prime pork banger and they turned and tottered away.

**

Today cycled to Ditchling, which is a relentless uphill grind until you reach the panoramic view that spreads out from Ditchling Beacon. Then it is pell mell downhill, winding, laughing until you reach the village itself, a vibrant little place full of shops and pubs, with parish council notices all over the place and a little museum plonked inside the graveyard. Famished, I set off the tinkling doorbell at 'Dolly's Pantry' where old-fashioned hospitality is served up in a sequence of cosy timbered rooms. A goodly number of locals dotted about the place, vociferously describing the tiniest detail of their lives, much relating to the precarious tightrope of old age. One kindly old codger was recounting how he'd taken a tumble at home, lay still, gingerly gathered his limbs about him and was relieved to discover nothing amiss beyond a sore ankle. Carried on his customary pursuits, visiting his daughter and the post office, but in the evening when bending down to rub whitchhazel into the tender ankle, his new hip joint popped out of place, and he was left immobilised in agony on the floor. Dragged himself to the phone and directed his neighbour to call 999. So tightly were his haunches locked, the hospital had to rip off his trousers with a pair of scissors. No anal sex for him that night. The nodding couple who'd absorbed the whole tale inquired if he'd ever thought of moving to somewhere where help was at hand. They were of the opinion it was better to undergo the trauma of moving house while body and soul were still sturdy. I enunciated a crisp grunt of assent and tinkled out of the door.

**

Luxurious days float by like golden autumn leaves. Set off on the train that scuttles between the coastal encampments West of Brighton. Half hedgeclipped suburbia and birdsong. Half the socially underfed-illiterate graffitti, ancient parkas, crumpled mouths on lopsided faces. The roll call of stations read like a Sussex version of the Weather Report.

'Portslade; Fishersgate; German Byte;

Lancing; Sompting; Goring on Sea'.

Terry Garogan, resident comic at The Crocodile Club, famously transformed the Trogs 'Wild Thing' into 'Lancing... you make my heart sing'. George Harrison was inspired by 'Sompting', and matadors everywhere have a soft spot for Goring.

Alighted at Shoreham and ventured along the River Adur. All rather flat and uneventful until I crossed the churchyard at Coombes, up through closely contoured woodland to a hilltop view at Cross Dyke where I got locked into a staring match with a black-faced sheep. Circled the brim of Steyning Bowl and then hurtled down to the village below, almost knocking over Miss Marple. Steyning, pronounced Stining by local folk, gives way to Bramber and then Upper Beeding, all resplendent in bloom and snug old pubs. Had a bowl of cauliflower soup in one pub, a pint of Tanglefoot in the next, and then was back along the River Adur. An old carmudgeon with a voice of parchment asked if I knew that bikes were banned from the footpath. Secretly wishing to club him with a mace and hang him from the ramparts at Bramber castle, I meekly answered 'No'. The path ended at a thundering road, but luckily a professional biker in helmet and padded gloves, lead me through a hole in the hedge and a secret track to Shoreham, bordered here and there with huge and happy sculptures.

This time of leisured bliss has gone on far too long.

'You're looking remarkably well', people ask in

accusation. 'What are you actually <u>doing</u> now?'

'Oh, a bit of this and that', I reply nonchalantly, twisting the exasperation screw one notch tighter. For just £2.20 per day I have the freedom of Brighton buses, and have become an afficianado of municipal travel. The drivers tend to be pantingly obese, dire shapeless bosoms squashed beneath regulation shirt. Just about able to summon the obligatory wave to an oncoming bus. Principal patrons are game old ducks who sparkle with delight once installed in their seat, and multiple mothers, tatooed and terrible, roaring out threats to their unruly brood. 'Right, there'll be no cigarettes for your tea tonight!!' It can all be such contagious fun, until that is, you get stuck next to a seriously stinking person ringing out the chimes on their mobile phone. At such moments you long for a smooth, liveried, cushioned bus, the conductor primed to bar adults who dribble and manic sprogs. 'Sorry love, there's a Knackered Carriage just behind'.

***

The train trundled in past a tennis court set in the grounds of an old ruined priory. And this is Lewes, history town, a castle up on the hill, Anne of Cleves House, even the open air pool is the oldest in England, bubbling up from a Spring. The streets clamber over the Downs. Cross the river past Harveys Brewery and you hit a steep hill which looks out onto the whole town, a little inland harbour and the railway tracks running alongside the Ouse. Tread the creaking, cosy corridors of the White Hart Hotel, and you come to a conservatory with a private view of the hills.

The hollow of the town has a lovely park filled with peace and exquisite old houses. A sleepy hollow, Lewes has all the old shops and trades of a time gone by. It comes to life just once a year on Guy Fawkes Night when an effigy of the Pope is carried through the town, rockets and bangers flying horizontally through the air amid scenes of medieval mayhem.

The lure of Lewes can mean only one thing. Encroaching Middle Age. Not as in the time when Simon de Montfort defeated Henry II up on the hill. But that period of life when you feel content to be in a place with chocolate shops and gentlemans' outfitters, but no semblance of life once dusk descends. Church Twitten, Thebes Gallery, polished solicitors nameplates more absurd than anything Dickens could conjure. The Crown Inn, solid wood-panelled watering hole of the County Court where the beak might inadvertently hand down five years or ten, or, with both of us hanging on an infinite silence, pronounce that Billy should be sent to a hospital instead.

A little way south, Rodmell lies in a rare swathe of flat land between three corners of the Downs. Smoke from the pub chimney floats along a single street of worn slate roofs and lattice windows. Every now and then a local artist throws open their Howards End to public view. You tiptoe through an interior of exquisite beams and china, and peek into a garden with a light and spacious outhouse you would happily call home. Several of the exhibits have been set aside, 'Polly' – not for sale, likewise 'Mr and Mrs Lloyd Bostock', settling whimsical and chinless into comfortable old age. One favourite subject is depicted in several moods, 'Pepita pensive', 'Pepita vacant', 'Pepita voluptuous on the chaise longue'. Over a stile at the end of the village, past the customs post, you are into a corrugated working farm. Disconnected bits of machinery strewn about the place, the obligatory tyre mountain and a car marooned in the long grass, each window inscribed in dripping paint, 'Scum! Scum! Scum!' Head on to the river bank leaving the silent rage behind. Right along the Ouse, past serene clusters of sheep and swans, out towards the sea. Boarded the boat one more time for Normandy, the final act in the judicial saga, Monsieur Mule versus the Nasty coffee company. A wonderful performance of rising and sitting where even the lady lawyers are referred to as 'Maître' or master. Perhaps the scenario of a Maîtresse flouncing about the court, sweeping aside her robe to reveal a strapping stockinged leg, garter and nifty little cane, would be more than the French Republic could allow. In the event, nothing unduly distracted the judges from their gentle reverie. They rose, sough the advice of the chief lackey and shuffled off for an early bath.

Stepped out into the soft sunshine to retrace the steps of my former routine. Comfortable corners of familiar cafés. The dear old Maghreb couscouserie, whitened window pane signaling its demise. The little parade of shops where every transaction is couched in a medley of greeting and farewell. The walled garden of the Musée Céramique, a private oasis of calm hidden in the heart of the city. Ending where I began, at the Hôtel Normandya, tiny toilet door secreted in the winding stairwell, lights cutting in mid-flight to save a precious centime. Forty years of folding and ironing sheets, Madame is now a little the worse for wear. She ushered me into the office furnished in the quiet comfort of a gentler age, and offered a graphic discourse on her newly-acquired knee. Outside, banners were unfurling in the Cathedral square, in protest against the drift to war. The seried ranks of stone faces, recently restored to their crannies on the tower, looked down on the crowd below and nodded in benediction.

***

What changes have there been in Brighton the two years I've lived away?

Well there's a new subtlety to the Queen Scene with the opening of 'Kruze' and 'Fuk'. Apparently they toyed with the idea of 'Splice my buttock with a luminous woggle', but the signwriter ran out of space. And there's a trend for fat girls to go around in shrunken tops, wads of stomach battened down with body metal, trousers sagging below the hairy shoreline. All just about bearable until a waitress wobbles up to take your cappuccino order, belly button bulging in your face.

Another novelty is the omnipresence of 'absolutely' in everyday speech. Previously the preserve of genial old buffers in gentlemans clubs, emerging from reverie, vaguely aware of the need to contribute something to the conversation, they would bluster 'Absolutely', deftly administer a thumbful of snuff to the old beak, and then lapse back into the mists of time. Now 'absolutely' is everywhere, breaking through the hubub of a pub, singsong delivery hinging on the emphatic 'lute' syllable. Big brassy seagulls, break off from chimney pot duty to plunder a lone bin bag, drain a pile of crumpled beer cans, settle down among the debris, webbed feet tucked inside snazzy braces, and confide in sozzled seagull patter, 'Isn't life sweet Sidney?'.

'Yes. Absolutely'.

And The Dome has reopened after a multi million facelift, new world concert hall for our bid to be City of Culture. Originally the stables of the Prince Regent, horses used to canter in sequence round the stalls, a chorus line in the orchestra pit beating time with their hooves. Now the upper apex of the dome is revealed through a sheen of glass, and I sit in cool comfort watching a performance of drum and danse. A far cry from the old days when you used to drop in and out of a classical concert, wilting in the heat. The sense of torpor intensified by the immense age of the average Philarmonic fan. It would all begin brightly, the faithful entranced by Barry Wordsworths' energy and wayward hair, but by the end the audience had ossified, and it would take an interminable hour for all the paraphenalia of old age to click in, and a sclerotic conga head off up the aisle to the foyer. Here too breathtaking renovation. What was once the Town Library, now a magnificent bar and palatial toilet suite. The new library will need tumbling water and pineapple plants to compete.

Once upon a time the identity of the place was clear. Brighton alive, two nightclubs per head of population and the biggest Festival in the land. Hove, shrouded in net curtains, derived from the ancient Danish for a burial ground. Well now, by some gruesome process of genetic manipulation, we are all one, congealed together as 'The City of Brighton and Hove'. I no longer know who I am.

***

All these years in Brighton and never once penetrated the campus at Sussex University. Well all that changed today, the 25 bus tip-toed over the humps, through the curtain of trees, and there it was, a vast city of learning nestling under the Downs. Thousands of people milling from lecture to cafeteria, effortlessly manipulating text, walkman and chewing gum in a bubble of their own.

I read every page on the noticeboard, waiting to be interviewed for the job of pastry chef. A perfectly round head chef and a dapper catering officer gently fired questions about gelatinous mousses and gluten-free cakes, and I wondered what meandered through their minds. Climbed the bus back to town and tuned into the conversation behind. Three freshers languidly exchanging smalltalk about soaps, next Tuesdays' tutorial, and writing a letter to nan. Surely these polished pups do not possess a 'nan'. Nanny more like, but in the great modern melting pot that reduces us all to one, they growl their words from the back of the throat and blunt their cut glass accents. What goes on during weekends home? Does that lazy rebel drawl cause the crystal to shiver at dinner? 'Tthhrree Edmund, three! Free is quite a different concept.' Or do they scorch back up the drive avid to reclaim their birthright. 'Nanny!! Edmondo's home! Marmite soldiers, marmite soldiers, where's my riding crop?!?'

Returned to the Mulehouse for a serious snooze prior to bonfire night. Vaguely aware of the world outside dissolving in a crescendo of pounding rain, eliminating any prospect of roasted chestnuts and jacket spuds charred in the glowing embers. Still the fridge was bursting with fodder; lentil apricot and cardamon soup, cod and aioli bagels, and light apple tartlets. Around midnight the rain lifted to a warm mist hanging on the lamposts. We ventured into the garden and set light to the Co-Op assortment of pyrotechnic delights, ending with a Catherine wheel that was all pent up energy but no movement, a terrible stammerer unable to break into speech, the coiled fuse simply searing into the post that props up the garden shed. Coincidentally, the man next door set off a Catherine Wheel that swirled like a ballerina in a pool of phosphorescent light. The contrast between Margot Fonteyne and my stillborn dud unleashed a wave of merriment, Fishwife Carol recounting how trying to be helpful in a casualty department, she crushed a womans crutch in the wheel of her chair. 'And when you say you crushed her crutch in the chair...' Pierre broke off, pounding his fists into the sodden grass.

Perhaps it is the years of dirt and danger, but Brighton fishing folk have little time for social niceties. A local history recounts how a fisherman set down his wheelbarrow outside a house one night and shouted up 'Widow Miller! Widow Miller'. The window shot up indignantly, 'I am not Widow Miller.' Nodding at the heap in the barrow the man said, 'You are now'. A few old survivors of the trade rampage along the front in their supercharged chairs, and settle in a cluster around Carol's stall, staring out to sea.

***

The Duke of Yorks, oldest cinema on the South Coast, limped along for years projecting arthouse images to a handful of paying guests. Rain came in through a crater in the ceiling, the seats were chaotically sprung and the projectionist just about kept the show on the road midst whirring spools and spindles. Either side of the giant screen the toilets read Pearl and Dean. Hapless offerings, excruciating as a Swedish comedy, were interspersed with little gems that left you purring and renewed. A scene from 'Tale of the Gypsies', with lantern lit fishing boats becalmed on a quivering delta. Insights to the meaning of life vapourised as you emerged from the darkened womb to the roar of Preston Circus. Despite the famous allnighters when the horror show rocked, the Duke was living on borrowed time. Then new owners took control, the ceiling was plugged, the old torn raffle ticket gave way to internet access and the obligatory café opened upstairs. The place is humming now and there is word of extending next door to make a multiscreen for sophisticats. Do not do this thing. Too much of Brighton has been made clean and swish. All that is wholesome and ramshackle is now under threat.

Returned to 'Club Revenge' for the first time in an age. The same neon view of the pier and the carpet deep in stickiness. Ten years ago Peter Glenton introduced Billy and Robbie, both big-eyed at the bar, and so began the summer of 'Please Don't Go', the history of the Mules. The thunderous night we towelled each other down with bar mats when rain cascaded through the roof. The cabaret act who awarded Billy a banana, the taste lingering all night. We introduced innocent Beulah to our coterie of queens, raised her on a pedestal showered her with fairy dust, and embraced her with chivalry as her carriage did await. Tonights' young chickens, skimpy and thin, all seemed cosseted by big bosomed fag hags, staking out the dance floor to an infectious Latin beat.

There are so many camp corners to this town, as

one fades another emerges. 'Abracadabra' was a little brasserie below the railway bridge presided over by Bruno, rotund waistcoat and immaculate bow tie. One wall filled with ornaments pirated from Blackgang Chime or the fair. The other lined with testimony to Brunos clairvoyant prowess. Although he twittered like a bird in the normal course of service, engage the man in your future and a veil of serious intent would descend his face, portender of breathtaking perception. The cooking half of the operation unfortunately fell away, black-eyed bean stew lost its zest, the cakes got stale, and in a puff, 'Abracadabra' was gone.

A mile South as the crow flies is The Cricketers pub, a little catacomb of snugness run for centuries by a bevy of ancient ladies who adorned the horseshoe bar in sparkling pearls and baubels. Upstairs in a highwaymans parlour, they dished up boiled beef and carrots and roly poly puds. Winnie and the girls have long since departed, but the same solid fare can be had in the supremely shlock surrounds of the Regency Tavern, glowing peroxide waiters welcoming and chivvying the customers along.

Next stop on my chefing tour of Brighton, an elderly residential home secured by an intrepid intercom that left me marooned beneath a haemorrhaging sky. The Churchill House Activity Centre. Just pondering what this might entail – absailing, body piercing, Tae Kwon Do, when the shackles clicked free and I was inside an atmosphere of antiseptic and piss, the aroma intensified by nuclear powered heating. A harassed carer pointed me towards the kitchen where all the equipment lay shrouded in muslin. No sign of the head cook, but a crumpled photo on the window ledge revealed her pretty as a bulldog. She did not appear all day, presumably slipped a disc stirring a vat of savoury mince. Managed to put together a meal of roast chicken for the active residents and lentil bake for the staff, and left hopeful that the rain might banish the pungency from my pores.

Then onto the University kitchen that generated remarkably fine food and blokish banter personified by Boris the Turkish porter, lumbering gait, bearlike arms, 'Innit' implanted in his speech. Decided to supplement the chefing with waiting too, so set off in search of a black bow tie. There is a second hand clothiers at the top of Church Road, everything from top hat and tails to gendarme caps and trench coats. G&K Rosen established 1918. The proprietor watched from the doorway as I parked my bike, and insisted on bringing his ties into the street lest my trusty stead be stole. He must have uttered the word 'Sir' a hundred times, recorded the transaction in a dogeared book, and then divulged his takings for the day. 'Very well worth it sir, very well worth it.' He counselled me on the wisdom of a cycle helmet and gently bowed farewell.

Just below the University is Stanmer Park, a little fold in the Downs tapering to a line of stone cottages, a tea room and a church with fading tombstones where the locals 'fell to sleep'. The Downs sweep on into town, cresting along Moulescoomb, upto the racecourse, then down to the Deaneries running out to sea. Turn about and the seried streets of Brighton clamber over the hills, two imperial viaducts bissecting the sky. The Royal Pavilion shares this sense of space, nothing impinging on its turbans and minarets. Best seen at night from the 'Blue Parrot' balcony, powerful cocktails shimmying the silouhette.

**

The little train that shuttles off to the Marina has been granted a winters' rest, and the stalls and sideshows along the way are accumulating rust. One night Billy gave me a private ride on the merry go round, then scampered up the big wheel, hanging from each girder on his way to the top. Vast dilated pupils set in a sculpted face, lured me into the turmoil of his life. How suddenly spontaneity could tip into despair. Body limp, inkwell eyes, a phrase stuck in distress. Come down my fragile beauty let me sooth you in my nest, let me rub away the hallmark of neglect. The litany of children's homes, the shifting sands of care.

Our first summer we splashed about in The Aquarium pub, one of many watering holes at the bottom of St. James Street. This one risen out of the ordinary by a maestro known as 'Moist'. We might dance to Deans' music till the vinyl scratched, or hurtle about the bar like Groucho Marx. Of course

Moist did not inherit his name at birth. One sticky summers day he trapsed upto our barstools and laboriously unfurled 'It's just so moist,' the lisp hanging in the air. Occasionally he mounted a costume epic at the end of the tiny bar, fashioned from his own needle and thread.

Tonight a Christmas performance at 'Café Prague'. A once in a while cabaret hosted by Barb Jungr, a warm ebullient presence, nurturing local talent and mingling with the guests. First up, a cocksure girl in a Santa outfit, oblivious to the ineptitude of her act. Then a corduroy couple of clean cut boys, drain the life from a Beatles song, and trip off to hoover the flat. Just when it seems the Blue Angel has fallen from its tree, a young man unfurls a voice so tremulously husky, rekindling the sensation of forgotten fruit. Finally, Barb commands the room with ease, lips puckering, prowling eyes, sparkling scarlet vest. The lesbian contingent on heat.

Every now and then Brighton takes to the streets to celebrate the Eclipse, the Millennium, Seagulls success, always gravitating towards the sea. Now the winter solstice means the Burning of the Clocks. The procession fills the Pavillion grounds, hundreds of candlelit lantern clocks swaying in the breeze, a magnificent peacock, a white seahorse, Mother Earth embracing the sun. Off towards the Colonnade, a stretch of promenade untouched by passing time, no Fatboy sounds or organic tea, just a grandstand view of the sea. A giant clockface ripples with flame, sparklers spinning upon each hour, like cossack dancers possessed. Rockets soar and shatter to the pounding of hooves and drums, long lines of surf marching in from the night.

***

That first venture to Rouen, Billy should have come too. We traced his birth certificate with the inscription of unknown roots. Then came a passport, but mercurial as ever, he failed to appear at the boat. Returning from the trip, an uneasy feeling stirred in the pub; did you know, while you were away.... I ran off gulping in the rain, upto the hospital, impenetrable at night, a shaft of light led me in and onto the ward, the curtain parting to reveal a charcoal stained white T-shirt, gills a little grey, slight figure of life, monitor beeping away. Two days later he was plugged into the hospital phone, savouring the drama like a puppy with a bone.

Chambreavervue